INCLUDING CHILDREN IN WORSHIP

A Planning Guide for Congregations

Elizabeth J. Sandell

Augsburg   Minneapolis

Dedicated with love to
Amanda Beth Leonard and Karen Ruth Leonard,
who have taught me about involvement in worship.

INCLUDING CHILDREN IN WORSHIP
A Planning Guide for Congregations

Scripture quotations unless otherwise noted are from the Holy Bible, New International Version. Copyright © 1973, 1978, 1984 International Bible Society. Used by permission of Zondervan Bible Publishers.

Cover illustration: David LaRochelle
Interior: RKB Studios Inc.

Library of Congress Cataloging-in-Publication Data
Sandell, Elizabeth J.
     Including children in worship : a planning guide for congregations
  / by Elizabeth J. Sandell.
        p.   cm.
     Includes bibliographical references.
     ISBN 0-8066-2544-9
     1. Children in public worship.   2. Worship (Religious education)
I. Title.
BV26.2.S25   1991
264'.0083—dc20   91-4375
                                                                      CIP

The paper used in this publication meets the minimum requirements of American National Standard for Information Sciences—Permanence of Paper for Printed Library Materials, ANSI Z329.48-1984. ∞™

Manufactured in the U.S.A.   AF 9-2544
                                                        15 14 13

CONTENTS

PREFACE

I take great pleasure in expressing gratitude to the many persons whose contributions add to the richness of this book and whose work inspired, encouraged, and corrected me at many times. I especially want to thank the men, women, girls, and boys who were involved at St. John's Methodist Church, Davenport, Iowa, where I grew up; at the Evangelical Covenant Church of North Mankato, Minnesota, where I came to know Jesus Christ; and at First Covenant Church, St. Paul, Minnesota, Crosstown Covenant Church, Minneapolis, Minnesota, and Roseville Covenant Church, Roseville, Minnesota, where my husband and I have ministered with children, youth, and adults.

Colleagues who have encouraged, collaborated, and contributed in the ministry of involving children in congregational worship have my warm gratitude. These include Rev. Bruce Lawson, Dr. Frances M. Anderson, Susan Chelgren Peterson, Mary Carlson Tornquist, Rev. Melanie Tornquist, Rev. Karen Palmatier, Rev. William Johnson, Arlen Hviding, Victoria Wilson, Rev. Tim Johnson, Dr. Marjorie L. Oelerich, Dr. Eugene C. Kreider, Beverly Bergstrom, Steven Goodenberger, Harry and Bonnie Opel, Margaret and Baxter Swenson, Lois Brokering, Marilyn Stalheim, Rev. Steve Burger, Martha Burger, Rick and Pat Carlson, Colleen and Scott Deery, Penny Zettler, Dr. William L. Peterson, Jr., Rev. J. Christopher Icenogle, Rev. Carleton Peterson, Judy Buer Peterson, Rev. Wendy Sorvik, Rev. Austin Kaufmann, and Rev. Duane Cross.

To my editors at Augsburg, Irene Getz and Lois Torvik, I want to express warm thanks for their encouragement, creativity, and patience.

Finally, I give very special thanks to my husband, Dennis, for his encouragement and understanding and self-sacrifice.

ACKNOWLEDGMENTS

"I Am the Church! You Are the Church!" by Richard Avery and Donald Marsh. Copyright © 1972 by Hope Publishing Co., Carol Stream, IL 60188. All rights reserved. Used by permission.

"Built on a Rock" (*LBW* 365), Nikolai F. S. Grundtvig; tr. Carl Doving, adapt. Copyright © 1958 *Service Book and Hymnal.*

"Order for an Agape Feast" adapted from *The Worshipbook: Services and Hymns,* copyright © 1970, 1972 The Westminster Press. Adapted and used by permission of Westminster/John Knox Press.

Luke 2:1-7 in German from *Die Bibel in heutigem Deutsch,* copyright © 1982 Deutsche Bibelgesellschaft Stuttgart.

Luke 2:1-7 in French from *La Bible en francais courant,* copyright © 1982 Societe biblique francaise.

Material on "Blessings for Children at Communion" used by permission of Duane Cross.

Excerpts from "Children and Adults: Partners in the Worshipping Community" from *The Covenant Companion,* July 1987, copyright © 1987 Covenant Publications, Chicago, IL 60625. Used by permission.

Material for the activity "The Lord's Prayer" and for "Liturgical Dance" used by permission of Vickie Wilson.

Material for "Musical Instruments" used by permission of Susan L. Peterson.

Material for "Processions" used by permission of Susan L. Peterson and Margie Swenson.

Material for "Bible Drama" and "Puppets and Music" used by permission of Margie Swenson.

Material for "Banners" used by permission of Martha Burger.

"Can You Count the Stars?" Text: Traditional Music: Traditional; arr. Mary Tornquist. Arrangement copyright © Mary Tornquist. Used by permission.

Lord's Prayer prepared by the International Consultation on English Texts.

1 WHY INCLUDE CHILDREN IN WORSHIP

Worship in the Christian church usually has an adult orientation. It is created by adults for adults, although children may occasionally participate as choir members, acolytes, or other helpers. Nevertheless, the spoken Word and the words of the hymns and the worship service seldom use the average child's vocabulary, sentence structure, images, and life experiences.

The question to be asked by all congregations is whether children should be included, excluded, or simply disregarded in the act of corporate worship. The question exists whether or not we verbalize it. It is often answered by default—by continuing practices with which the adult membership is familiar and comfortable but which seldom relate to the experience level of children.

Including Children in Worship has been prepared after much thought, observation, experience, prayer, and research. It assumes that when we baptize or dedicate a child into the family of God, that child has a meaningful place in what that family does as a group, including worship. Another underlying assumption is that people of all ages belong in the worshiping community. Children should be involved in worship with adults because the church follows Jesus Christ, assumes responsibility for children at their dedication or baptism, and is designed as a covenant community. Surely children, as God's creation, are part of that community. How, then, do they experience this community? How do they perceive it? How do adult members of the congregation carry out the promises made at the baptism or dedication service?

This book supports the belief that children do belong in the congregational worship setting as full and participating members of that community at worship: children do want to worship.

A mother told the story of her five-year-old who challenged the pastor occasionally on their way out of church. One Sunday, it was: "Why didn't you pray for my friend who is in the hospital?" Another Sunday, it was: "Did you mean the angels in heaven or the Los Angeles Angels?" Children do listen.

Children are learners. Adults, too, are learners and can learn even from children. Children belong in the worship service as ministers, a true part of the priesthood of believers who can also enrich the learning of parents and other adults as they worship. Those who do not have children especially need to observe them, even when their behavior is distracting. Children can show us what it means to become "as a little child." Children may be dependent, but they can also be loyal, amazingly honest, spontaneous, eager, and completely involved. We see in them how childlike characteristics can be put into action. They show us our need to continue the journey of faith.

Children are learners. The questions need to be asked: What are children learning during the worship service that will support faith development? What do children learn about themselves, about the world, about the church, and about God in the worship setting? How will this be reflected in their adult faith—or lack of faith? If children belong in worship, how do we include them in a way that affirms who they are and how God made them to be?

Some congregations provide a separate children's church-time program for young children. Such programs might offer opportunities for worship that are appropriate to the children's level of development through creative teaching methods, such as drama, puppets, and music. A separate children's church-time might enable parents to participate more completely in the adult worship experience. But the separate children's church-time divides the family—and the congregation—as a worshiping group. Adults might develop an attitude that keeps children in their separate place so that adults are not distracted from their worship. Although it may be unintentional, such programs can become simply babysitting for the convenience of adults and worship leaders.

A church's worship committee was considering what to do with children in worship. Children usually stayed with the congregation until just before the sermon. Then the children left the sanctuary for their own group time. Recruiting leadership and finding curriculum that was easy to prepare for this "children's church" became problems. Adults were "too busy" to commit to a role that would take them away from the main worship service on a regular basis. And most curriculum materials seemed more like Sunday school curriculum. Was "children's church" to be an educational experience or a scaled-down version of adult church?

The worship committee discussion went something like this: "What curriculum should we use? Extended Sunday school lessons? Games and puppets? Bible stories? Free choice of arts and crafts and table games?"

"We should select curriculum based on the goals for children's church. But what are the goals for children's church?"

"The goal should be to help children learn how to worship."

"Are games and puppets worship? Is children's church really worship at the children's level, whatever their level is?"

"Why shouldn't children attend congregational worship? Couldn't they attend 'big church' to worship with their families? Wouldn't they learn from observing adults at worship? Why is children's church separated from 'big church'?"

"Children's church allows adults to worship quietly and without disturbance. The pastor doesn't want his sermon interrupted."

"How do children learn to worship? By learning to sit still? Is sitting still worship?"

"But, can children worship?"

"What is worship, anyway?"

The last question is really the starting point. Leaders should be clear about worship itself before considering the role of children in worship.

Worship is a community action in which adults and children can participate. The message of the gospel suggests that the good news is for all ages. The church includes persons of all ages, and God seeks and accepts worship from young and old alike.

Christian education and worship are closely related: worship leads us to, and is supported by, the programs of Christian education. In worship, we praise and adore God. To communicate fully with God, we soon want and need to learn more about God. In education, we learn about who God is and about God's purpose for humankind. As we understand more, we worship God even more deeply.

Adults who guide worship experiences can develop many opportunities to include children in the worshiping congregation. Involvement in corporate worship will give children another opportunity to discover answers to their questions, such as: Why do you think God hears us pray? Why is the Bible difficult to understand? Who made God? These are profound and important questions. Children deserve to be taken seriously and incorporated into the worshiping community. When the worship leaders communicate about faith in language suitable for children, they model conversation that parents can use at home.

Pastors and staff in small and large churches, as well as members of boards or committees for education and worship, are looking for creative ways to involve worshipers in response to God. When a congregation is composed of individuals of all ages, this can challenge even the most creative and dedicated worship leaders.

This book is developed in order to give pastors and others involved in planning congregational worship some suggestions and guidelines for including young children in worship experiences. Here we propose to examine what our approach to worshiping with children can be; how to plan for congregational worship to account for the ways children think and develop; and some very practical, concrete ways that have been used successfully to include children in worship.

For purposes of this resource, the word *children* will be defined as including youngsters between birth and eight years of age, and most of the material is focused on including these children in congregational worship. This book includes some suggestions for involving older children and youth as well.

When children see people of a variety of ages involved in worship, they will actually experience how worship can include everyone, that everyone can worship, and that God seeks praise from all persons. Young children and adults need to participate in worship with people of all ages, with all types of learning styles, with all sorts of self-expression, and with all kinds of talents and abilities. God seeks worship and praise from everyone.

Let us here acknowledge two important points: first, the role of the pastor and, second, the young child's need for movement.

The pastor's role is critical in planning worship that involves all ages as participants in praising God. It is the pastor who can coordinate all the elements of worship so that adults and children are actually lifting their praises to God, rather than forming an audience for a "program." Pastors and worship leaders must be theologically responsible. The material presented in this resource is intended to enhance the worship experience, to encourage people of all ages to praise God, and to build the community of faith.

Secondly, young children do need movement. Members of the congregation will want to be realistic about the amount of activity that can be tolerated in the sanctuary pews. However, it may be this very characteristic that children can contribute to the corporate worship experience. The Bible describes worship in physical terms: standing, kneeling, lifting hands, lifting the head, clapping hands, dancing, lying down, wearing sackcloth. These all can reflect and encourage an attitude of praise and worship. These are all positions that children will enthusiastically try. Furthermore, allowing children freedom of movement just might release their natural gifts for ministry. Dennis Benson and Stan Stewart tell this story:

"As I ponderously launched into my third point, a small toddler left his parents in a pew toward the back and made his way down the aisle. At the fourth row from the front he paused, turned, and climbed on the seat. He sat there beside her [a woman who had just learned that she had cancer]. I don't think he said anything, just snuggled in. Her arm encircled him. He responded with a hug. He sat with her for only a minute or so, and then he went back to his parents. But, my God, her face! I saw it. Warmth and hope once again lived in her eyes, courage shone in her bearing. She had received her gospel for the day" (Benson and Stewart 1978, 30).

STATEMENTS OF BELIEF ABOUT INCLUDING CHILDREN IN WORSHIP

The statements that follow have been developed in order to assist church leaders in articulating their own beliefs about their worshiping congregations. The statements might be used to start discussion about worship in general or about including children in particular or used to develop a brochure that describes to members and visitors the congregation's emphasis on including children in worship.

> Children of any age are welcome in our congregational worship services as participants with others of all ages.

> We include children in our congregational worship services because we are members of the *ekklesia,* the corporate body of Jesus Christ. We want to model God's design for a community where differences are accepted and affirmed and where individuals feel they belong.

> We include children in our congregational worship services because we follow Jesus Christ, who welcomed and fully accepted little children. We want to help children know that we, too, accept them as they are and that they can realize through experience the potential they have as children of God.

> We include children in our congregational worship services because we follow Jesus Christ, who directed his followers to learn from children. We need to have children

with us in order to observe and learn the qualities that Jesus Christ desired for his followers.

We include children in our congregational worship services because we believe in God, who directed believers to lead children. We need to have children with us in order for them to learn from the experiences of worship with the community of faith.

Therefore,

We will periodically review and reaffirm the value we place on the presence of children in our worshiping congregation.

We will establish a worship committee that will facilitate worship services in which people of all ages participate.

We will consciously invite children to join congregational worship services. We will schedule congregational worship separate from educational opportunities. We want the church family to worship together.

We will support parents in their role as their children's first and most important teachers about worship.

We will educate children about worship through the church's educational programs and, most importantly, through their experiences in congregational worship.

We will intentionally educate adults about worship through the church's educational programs and, most importantly, through their experiences in congregational worship.

2 As We Worship, So We Believe

What do adults believe about worship, the church, and the place of children in worship? Is worship an experience for adults *with* children? Or is congregational worship meant to be an adult experience *separate from* children?

Answers to these questions and others about the ways we enable children to worship with the family of God indicate how we view children and adults.

Are children an important and loved part of the church family? Are children welcomed and included along with adults? Or are children simply cute and entertaining? Are children capable of deep understanding and ministry? Do children have anything to contribute to enrich corporate worship? Or do children get in the way of adult worship?

WE LEARN TO WORSHIP

Leaders should be clear about worship itself before considering the role of children's worship. What is worship?

Worship is derived from the Anglo-Saxon "weorthscipe" or "worthy ship." To the Christian, it is a reverent response in thought, word, and deed to the supreme value of God's gift of Christ. Worship is central to our Christian faith. Worship is not for us, the people, but it is our service directed toward God through the words and actions of adoration, confession, thanksgiving, and commitment.

Worship consists of each person's individual thoughts and actions, usually combined in a group experience. The central nature of worship does not change with the age of the person involved.

Both the Old and New Testaments include illustrations about the importance of involvement of children in the life of the community.

WORSHIP IN THE OLD TESTAMENT

In the Old Testament, worship was generally for adult males. However, there are references to the role of children and to the image of children. Children were to be involved with the entire community in learning about God's relationship with the people. Young children were involved in significant ministry. The praise of all peoples would result in the world coming to know and praise God.

The Old Testament called God's people to involve the entire family in learning. In Deuteronomy 31:12-13, as the Hebrews approached the promised land, Moses commanded the people to assemble. All were to gather, including women, children, and strangers, so they could learn about God's law. Moses said, "Their children, who do not know this law, must hear it and learn to fear the Lord your God as long as you live in the land you are crossing the Jordan to possess."

Young children in Old Testament times were involved in significant ministry. For example, 1 Samuel 3 tells the story about the ministry of the boy, Samuel, before the Lord under the direction of Eli, a priest in the temple. The Lord called the boy, Samuel, into ministry and entrusted the boy with a prophecy about what was going to happen to Eli and his sons. In another example, the writer of 2 Kings 5 told about a young slave girl who suggested to Naaman's wife that if Naaman would see the prophet in Samaria, his leprosy would be cured. And 2 Chronicles 31:16-18 records that free-will offerings made to the Lord were distributed to the males, including males three years old, who would enter the temple of the Lord daily to perform their responsibilities.

The psalmist emphasized that it would be the praise of God by all peoples that would cause God's ways to be known among all nations. The result of carrying out this duty would be that others then would come to know and praise God: "May God be gracious to us and bless us and make his face shine upon us, that your ways may be known on earth, your salvation among all nations. May the peoples praise you, O God; may all the peoples praise you" (Psalm 67:1-3).

Writers and prophets of the Old Testament used the image of child or son to describe the relationship between God and God's people. This is a powerful metaphor that can draw out profound feelings and responses from those who hear it.

"But I have stilled and quieted my soul; like a weaned child with its mother, like a weaned child is my soul within me" (Psalm 131:2).

"For to us a child is born, to us a son is given, and the government will be on his shoulders. And he will be called Wonderful Counselor, Mighty God, Everlasting Father, Prince of Peace" (Isaiah 9:6).

"The wolf will live with the lamb, the leopard will lie down with the goat, the calf and the lion and the yearling together; and a little child will lead them. . . . The infant will play near the hole of the cobra, and the young child put his hand into the viper's nest. They will neither harm nor destroy on all my holy mountain, for the earth will be full of the knowledge of the Lord as the waters cover the sea" (Isaiah 11:6-9).

"I will extend peace to her [Jerusalem] like a river, and the wealth of nations like a flooding stream; you will nurse and be carried on her arm and dandled on her knees. As a mother comforts her child, so will I comfort you; and you will be comforted over Jerusalem" (Isaiah 66:12-13).

To describe someone as the son of someone else was to suggest that he belonged to that other person. Children illustrate these powerful metaphors. How will we be able to understand these images if the children are not with us?

WORSHIP IN THE NEW TESTAMENT

In the New Testament, the good news is available to everyone, male or female, Jew or Gentile, adult or child. The message was immediately personified by Jesus Christ's birth. In his ministry, Jesus himself directed his followers to bring children to know and praise him. Furthermore, in the New Testament the image of a child continues to be used as a powerful metaphor.

Perhaps most importantly, Jesus Christ was born on earth as an infant, personifying dependency and helplessness. At the birth of Jesus, Scripture records three beautiful songs, each one praising God for bringing Jesus Christ as an infant. Mary's song glorifies the Lord for his mercy toward the humble people (Luke 1:46-55). The angels' song praises God for the birth of a baby, now wrapped in cloths and lying in a manger (Luke 2:14). Simeon's song tells of his wonder and satisfaction upon seeing the child, in whom salvation will be accomplished (Luke 2:29-32).

Later, during his ministry, Jesus became indignant when the disciples tried to keep children away out of fear that they would disturb him. The disciples were blind to the worth of even the youngest ones. Jesus did not just scold adults for forbidding children to approach him; he rebuked them for *hindering* the children, for neglecting to bring them to himself (Luke 18:15-17).

In the New Testament, too, the image of a child is used as a metaphor for qualities necessary among Christians, particularly trust and receptivity. Jesus Christ said that anyone who will not receive the kingdom of God like a child will never enter it (Mark 10:13-16). Jesus welcomed spontaneous praise and worship and invited it from little children. As with the Old Testament images of children, how will we be able to understand these New Testament images if the children are not with us?

WE BECOME THE *EKKLESIA*

The church is designed to be the welcoming community that makes us unique, separate from the world as the worshiping congregation. The Christian church acknowledges together that we are the *ekklesia*, the corporate body of Jesus Christ. The whole family of God is "called out of" the world to be separate from the world in order to worship God. We are to meet in Christian fellowship, to love each other, to learn, to worship, and to nurture others in faith. We model God's design for a community where differences are accepted and affirmed, where individuals feel they belong.

This children's song reflects what the church really is meant to be:

I am the church! You are the church!
We are the church together!
All who follow Jesus, all around the world!
Yes, we're the church together!

And when the people gather
There's singing and there's praying,
There's laughing and there's crying sometimes,
All of it saying:

I am the church! You are the church!
We are the church together!
All who follow Jesus, all around the world!
Yes, we're the church together!

(Avery and Marsh, 1972)

CHILDREN COMPLETE THE FAMILY OF FAITH

When worship happens in the fellowship of faith, it becomes a celebration of belonging and participating in that community. We need children with us to complete the family of faith, to make it all that Jesus envisioned for the church. When we begin to include children, we also begin to be open to everyone, as Jesus commanded: the children, the poor, the powerless, the foreigners, the sinners. With a view of worship that includes children in significant ways, our words and actions communicate meaningfully with many different kinds of people, and we can truly become a community.

Because of our traditions and comfortable rituals, often our worship experiences separate the congregation from the rest of the world. We develop our own language and behavior. We understand and appreciate our meaning, but others may feel unwelcome and ignored. Attitudes that exclude children in worship may be clues that worship is closed to other groups as well. Churches that do not include children in meaningful worship may be ingrown and unwilling to include people different from themselves. One pastor commented: "Well, if we allow children to get involved in worship, then we'll hear from all kinds of other special interest groups. And that will just open a whole new can of worms!"

JESUS CHRIST WELCOMED CHILDREN

Jesus Christ blessed and welcomed little children even though his friends thought they were interruptions (Mark 10:13-15; Luke 18:15-17). Jesus cautioned his followers to accept children and not to hinder them. If we are going to follow Jesus' example, we will want to include children as well.

Young children may not directly recall the *words* of the sermon, but they may remember the experiences of belonging, acceptance, identification, enhanced self-worth, security, affection, mutuality, approval, and interdependence.

CHILDREN CAN EXPERIENCE FAITH

In the church, young and old belong together to share in the worshiping community with each other. John H. Westerhoff III in *Will Our Children Have Faith?* has suggested that it is critical that three generations be involved together in the faith community. Too often the church separates the generations in its programming and worship or completely ignores the older as well as the younger generation. The older generation is the generation of memory. The younger generation can be the generation of vision, but only if there is memory, which is provided by the older generation. The middle generation is the generation of the present, which confronts memory and vision with reality (Westerhoff 1983, 53-54). In an earlier book, Westerhoff emphasized that without interaction and sharing among the generations, the church cannot communicate its faith by *being* the community of faith, by offering to persons an *experience* of its message (Westerhoff 1970, 29).

There are several different views about how churches welcome children into the faith community. Some observe infant baptism; others practice the dedication or presentation of young children. Whatever a particular denomination believes, how children are involved in congregational worship services is an indication of how the members follow through on the statements they made during the infant dedication or baptism service.

For churches that practice infant baptism, the sacrament is considered to be a sign of belonging to the church, of welcome into the family of God. The words of the sacrament emphasize this belonging: "We welcome you into the Lord's family . . . as workers with us in the kingdom of God" (*Lutheran Book of Worship*, 121-125). "This sacrament, which is a sign of our cleansing, of our being joined to Christ, and of our welcome into the family of God . . ." (*The Covenant Book of Worship*, 90-96).

For churches that observe child dedication or presentation, the practice is a recognition of the importance of nurturing the child in the love and grace of God. "God grant that we all shall earnestly assume with these parents the responsibility for the Christian training of this child and all children" (Jesse Jai McNeil, *Minister's Service Book for Pulpit and Parish*, 52-54). ". . . by God's help, provide a Christian home for this child and bring him/her up in the worship and teaching of the Church" (*The Covenant Book of Worship*, 209-212).

CHILDREN CAN IDENTIFY WITH THE WORSHIPING CONGREGATION

The experiences that people have as children eventually will contribute to their behavior as adults. If children develop a sense of belonging with the family of faith, they may be more likely to want to maintain and increase their relationship and identity with the church and with God. If children feel unwelcome and out of place, they may want to sever their ties with the church.

In worship, children can develop their identity with the people of God. This feeling becomes a foundation for future participation in the ministry of the church and for a relationship with all Christians throughout the world.

WE CAN BUILD CHILDREN'S SELF-WORTH

When children are meaningfully involved in congregational worship, they can realize through experience the positive potential they have as children of God.

Favorable messages about a child's behavior may be interpreted by the youngster as affirmative statements about self and thereby reassure the child of God's love and care.

ADULTS CAN DEVELOP CHILDLIKE QUALITIES

In Matthew 18:1-4, Jesus refers to a child to illustrate the characteristics needed to enter the kingdom of heaven. Here is an expanded list of the important qualities of children.

joy	reconciliation
honesty	affirmation
receptivity	complete involvement
tenderness	motion and rhythm
awareness	clear communication
eagerness	expression of feelings
trust	energy
love	generosity
openness	acceptance
spontaneity	simplicity
hope	enthusiasm
imagination	creativity

Adults would be wise to bring these unassuming and genuine features to other roles in the church, such as fellowship, learning, and mission. Adults need to be willing to learn these attributes again from children, to be receptive to the childlike spirit that opens individuals to the gospel. When children worship with the congregation, adults may see this childlike nature in action.

CHILDREN CONTRIBUTE TO WORSHIP

Every one of us, young and old, can assist in the ministry of the church. Indeed, every one of us is *called* to assist in the ministry of the church. Messages and service do not come only from the pulpit. Nor do they come only from adults.

Every person, including every child, is given gifts to use to enrich the worship of the entire community. Children bring their complete involvement, their eagerness to participate, their laughter, their questions, and their imagination. Involving children creatively in worship can, in turn, cultivate the worship of others. For example, in a congregation of all ages, the use of sign language to interpret a hymn (see p. 44) may bring smiles to many faces. People become more animated and more likely to notice their neighbors and assist others as they try the signs.

Children can also minister to adults in worship. First, children contribute by their very presence. Everything is new to them, and they help us see God through their new eyes. They ask questions that help us clarify our beliefs and add energy to our own prayers to God.

Second, when children are included in congregational worship, adults can experience firsthand the strength of metaphors used in the Bible, as mentioned earlier. Statements about receiving the kingdom of God like a child have more power when children are present with us.

Remembering the Sunday worship service, five-year-old Missy met the pastor in the hall on the following Wednesday.

She grinned and said, "I liked the drama story last Sunday!"

"Wonderful!" the pastor thought. "Real learning must have happened during the Scripture interpretation that the older children presented last Sunday."

"What was the story about?" asked the pastor.

Missy thought a bit and then said, "Ummm . . . I forget. Something about God."

She didn't remember the details, but she did remember that there was a dramatic interpretation of Scripture that included and appealed to children. But there was more that she wanted to say.

"I hope you have another drama next Sunday . . . because I didn't get to be in the story last time."

Missy wanted to participate actively, to be part of what happened during worship.

CHILDREN DO WORSHIP

Can children worship?

Children worship with each new discovery of their lives: stars, puppies, and even snowflakes. Reverence, respect, love, awe, praise, adoration, appreciation, and honor come naturally to children. Jesus himself valued their songs of praise during his final week on earth.

In worship with the congregation, children will actively experience words such as these:

Hosanna: "Save us, we pray."

Hallelujah: "Praise (you) the Lord."

Shalom: wholeness, made perfect, peace.

Praise: to sing, to give glory to God.

Sofia Cavalletti, a Christian educator in Italy, has developed experiences for educational settings in which children can experience worship. She wrote in *The Religious Potential of the Child* that she has observed that all children experience God, whether or not they have structured religious education. Each child with whom she has worked has shown a spiritual inclination. As she shared Jesus' stories with youngsters, she observed their deep and spontaneous responses. Children expressed their experiences with God by their deep concentration and their expressions of joy and peace. Cavalletti is convinced that young children are not just getting *ready* to learn about God, but that they can actually know, love, and worship God in ways that are appropriate for their development and understanding. She emphasizes that children are not just *learning* about God through explanation and interpretation, but that children are *worshiping* through entering into the experience of the presence of God. The children are participating and "taking in" the experience (Cavalletti 1982).

CHILDREN SEEK TO BE INVOLVED IN WORSHIP

Children may seem to learn at random. They absorb information and feelings through every sense. For adults who do not understand how children learn and process their experience of worship, it seems easier to reprimand children who interrupt, to scowl at them, or to grumble than to receive them joyfully and respectfully, to explain the service, to enable them to participate, and to include them in the worshiping congregation.

Children want to know what is acceptable; they want help to understand our expectations. Behavior "problems" of children may actually be clues that leaders are too verbal or too intellectual, even for adults in the congregation. Children whisper and wiggle and drop papers. They naturally act as if the congregation should be seen and heard in worship. Young children can, in fact, learn to act appropriately when their active participation is welcomed and guided in love.

CONCLUSION

When we respond to God's call and become part of the *ekklesia,* the worshiping community, we may well decide to welcome children into congregational worship services. Jesus welcomed little children. Jesus directed his followers to become like little children. There is value both for children and adults in including children in worship services. Children can and do worship, and in worship, children can minister to the community.

God commanded believers to lead children into faith. We cannot exactly *teach* faith, but we can teach *about* faith and provide experiences that encourage faith development. For young children, participation in worship can become an experience of the faith community. Our response to God's direction should be to welcome and enable children to participate in the congregation's worship experiences.

3 WORSHIP IS CAUGHT, NOT TAUGHT

When a church believes that worship includes young children as well as adults, it is appropriate to develop strategies that will help implement this stance. These strategies may include reviewing attitudes about including children in worship, establishing a worship committee that will facilitate the inclusion of children in congregational worship, consciously inviting children to participate, supporting parent involvement, involving lay people in leading worship, and educating children about worship (all discussed in this chapter). Other strategies include developing adult programs to help them learn more about including children in worship (chapter 4) and responding to various concerns of church members (Appendix 1).

REVIEW ATTITUDES ABOUT WORSHIP

For worship to remain vital, the congregation should periodically review its stated attitudes toward worship. It is easy to continue forms and traditions of worship because "that's the way it's always been done" and it's comfortable. Too often, however, this complacency means that the service and music of worship are the focus of our worship. Instead, we must realize that God wants to be the center of our attention. God wants to receive worship that is alive and "spirited."

SEEK CONSISTENCY

Any statement the congregation writes should be consistent with the values the members hold and the kind of worship they seek to develop. For example, if the congregation values family-oriented worship that includes many different kinds of people, it would not want to send the children to a separate children's church time during the sermon on Sunday. It would be more consistent for the congregation to develop forms of worship that encourage children to participate along with their families.

With consistency of values in mind, this book does not advocate the use of children's sermons during worship even though some may be effectively done. Too often, children's "moments" become a time when the pastor tries to bring the message "down to the children's level," while only succeeding in providing a nice object lesson for the adults. Adults have been heard to say that they got more out of the children's time than they got out of the sermon. When this is true, it may mean that children got little or nothing out of the children's time, because the illustration was not concrete enough for them.

For example, when a pastor wanted to explain the Holy Spirit in a children's sermon, he inflated a balloon and remarked that the Spirit could fill people up like the air fills up a balloon. Some children misunderstood and became fearful that they might get so much of the Spirit that they would explode! Others thought that overweight people had an abundance of the Spirit. Even if children's sermons manage to be concrete enough for children, the time when the children come forward may actually exploit them. The congregation might be distracted by looking at the children, and the children might be distracted by looking at the congregation! This book advocates other, more creative, concrete, and meaningful ways to include children completely in worship.

QUESTIONS TO DISCUSS

In developing a statement about worship, church members will want to consider many questions. These may be discussed at an educational forum, at a retreat, by the church board, and by the worship committee.

1. What does worship mean? What does worship mean to our congregation?
2. Who is included in our worship experience? Who is excluded? Why is this true?

3. When do adults worship? When do children worship?

4. What do our Sunday school and other educational programs teach about worship? When do children learn about worship?

5. What do our families teach about worship? How are parents involved in worship?

6. How do adults learn? How do children learn?

7. Who leads our worship experiences? How does that model what we believe?

8. What do we want children to *know* about worship? What do we want children to *feel* about worship? What do we want children to *do* about worship?

ESTABLISH A WORSHIP COMMITTEE

WORSHIP COMMITTEE MEMBERSHIP

As you plan your worship committee, start by identifying people who value tradition but also appreciate innovation. Look for individuals who are flexible and cooperative and who can find resources and create ideas. This group might include the pastor, music leaders, educational leaders, several parents, several Sunday school teachers, the children's choir director, people who enjoy the creative arts, and others who care about children and families. In large congregations with many staff members, the ministers of education, youth, and music could be included.

This group might be a subcommittee of the church's education committee or the deacons. For ease of discussion, we will refer to this group as the worship committee.

WORSHIP COMMITTEE TASKS

Possible tasks of the worship committee might include:

1. List all scheduled worship services and experiences, and plan ahead to include children in each gathering. Build on existing traditions and celebrations. Be imaginative and creative.

2. Coordinate persons responsible for worship with activities in the Sunday school and children's choir.

3. Keep a record of the year's worship services, with copies of pictures, posters, banners, songs, stories, and other materials that were used.

4. Select special music for anthems, preludes, postludes, and hymns to include children.

5. Incorporate all senses naturally at logical moments in worship.

6. Compose and duplicate worship activity bulletins especially for children.

7. Write litanies and stories for worship that are appropriate for children's developmental levels.

8. Prepare family devotional material for special seasons.

9. Locate and purchase resources and supplies.

10. Write newsletter articles to explain how and why children are involved in worship and to emphasize that worship is participation rather than performance.

11. Write newsletter articles to give families advance notice of the worship themes and music so they can review these at home with their children.

12. Provide training for children and other lay persons who will be assisting with worship leadership responsibilities. Celebrate diversity. Use the people resources of the congregation.

13. Study relevant materials such as *Will Our Children Have Faith?* by John H. Westerhoff III (1983) or *The Ministry of the Child* by Dennis C. Benson and Stan J. Stewart (1978).

14. Consider the needs and willingness of the congregation to include children in worship in various ways.

15. Develop activities that involve children in worship as described in chapter 5, pages 31-69.

16. Meet regularly and evaluate the program. Build momentum slowly and pace the experiences. Avoid overloading the congregation.

INVITE CHILDREN TO PARTICIPATE

It is important that a congregation be intentional and clear about inviting children to participate in worship services.

SCHEDULE WORSHIP SEPARATE FROM EDUCATION

If the congregation values worship that includes children, it will not want to schedule education for children at the same time as the worship services. It is more consistent for the congregation to hold worship services at times when children can participate actively with their families.

ESTABLISH A CHILDREN'S WORSHIP TEAM

The worship committee might incorporate a children's worship team into its membership. The children's worship team would facilitate the involvement of children and youth in worship preparation and leadership. Together, adults and children might study the significance of worship and the biblical accounts of worship leaders in the Old Testament. For example, the worship leaders went before the Hebrews into battle. They also walked at the head of ceremonial parades. The worship team might learn and practice leading various parts of worship. They might prepare special contributions to worship, such as prayers, drama, or music.

COORDINATE CHILDREN'S EXPERIENCES

The worship committee can help coordinate worship education for children among the various church organizations. For example, during Sunday school opening exercises, a hymn and response can be taught that would also be used in that day's worship service. Or, in children's choir, youngsters can practice some parts of the worship service. These groups would also contribute their music or drama to the congregational worship experience.

The worship committee can also coordinate the ways of involving children in the congregation's worship services. For example, the committee could write the children's worship bulletins, in cooperation with the pastor(s). See chapter 5 for assistance.

SUPPORT PARENT INVOLVEMENT

Parents can welcome their children to worship with them and use the experience to establish a foundation for their children's faith.

Parents are important role models for their children. First, they will want to model regular attendance at worship. And second, they will want to model appropriate, attentive, and involved behavior in worship. Research has shown that there is considerable evidence for parental influence on the beliefs and social attitudes of their children. In the 1960s, Ronald Goldman (1968) found that children who had parental support (demonstrated by parental church attendance) achieved significantly higher religious insights and concepts that those children who did not have parents who attended church. More recent researchers found that if parents have positive attitudes toward the church, it is likely that their children will have positive feelings about the church (Benson, Williams, and Johnson 1987). It may be that while children may regularly attend church in their early years, their eventual church attendance as adults is more likely to be determined by their parents' actual attendance patterns and modeling.

Parents can help their children:

1. to understand as much as possible about what happens during worship,
2. to participate in the worship experience, and
3. to make the worship time as positive as possible and have some alternate quiet activities available for times when the children are restless.

WHAT FAMILIES CAN DO

The following are suggestions for parents, other adults, and older brothers and sisters.

Discuss worship at home to prepare children for any change in the routine, such as a baptism or other special feature. Also, take time to answer questions about worship experiences.

Bring a children's Bible story book, colored pencils or crayons for drawing in the children's worship activity bulletins, and a favored blanket or doll.

Arrive in time to find a good place to sit. Sit near the front, if you can, to provide younger children with a better view of the chancel. Let your child stand and stretch during the hymns.

Give your child cues about what will happen next in worship. Children who can read will want to find the hymns. They like to be ready. Help them follow along.

Express your gladness at having children in worship. After the service, be sure to welcome the children near you. Include them in your conversations to let them know they belong.

Free yourself from worry about children's behavior. Be open to receiving their ministry to you. Usually, children's restlessness is less disturbing to others than it is to you.

RESOURCES FOR PARENTS

The worship committee can provide a wide variety of resources that will help parents lead their children's involvement in worship.

1. A folder of suggestions for how parents can help children worship. (See chapter 5)
2. Weekly suggestions for family devotions printed in the children's worship activity bulletin.
3. Family devotional guides for use during the seasons of Advent or Lent.
4. Resource books to help families plan special worship times at home.
5. Special worship services at church identified as family worship times that involve children in even more active ways, such as at Thanksgiving.
6. Audiotapes of hymns, songs, and worship music.
7. Resource books to explain colors and symbols of worship.

A PARENT EDUCATION SESSION

Parent education sessions might be held several times each year for parents of newborns or parents of children who have recently been dedicated or baptized. These sessions can focus on ways to nurture faith in the home and at church. While examining their own responsibilities, parents can consider ways they may begin their own faith traditions at home.

An outline for such a session might include:

1. Welcome everyone and introduce the leaders.
2. Review the congregation's attitude toward including children in worship.
3. Teach about the stages of child development.
4. Teach about the stages of faith development; how children understand and participate in worship.
5. Watch the film, *The Mouths of Babes*, Tom Christensen (Director and Producer). Mass Media Ministries, 2116 North Charles Street, Baltimore, MD 21218, phone (301) 727-3270. This film also is available from Augsburg Fortress, Audiovisual Department, 426 South Fifth Street, Box 1209, Minneapolis, MN 55440.
6. Consider the relation of home worship and congregational worship.
7. Examine biblical models of family worship, in which parents are the interpreters of the faith.
8. Review the folder of suggestions for how parents can help children worship at home and at church.
9. Respond to questions.

INVOLVE LAY PEOPLE IN LEADING WORSHIP

The Christian church is an assembly of believers, and all are exhorted to participate in the priesthood. The worship committee can help to prepare individuals in the congregation for their own responsibilities in worship. Full participation in worship is a skill that can be developed. We build an awareness of God; we learn about confession and prayer; we practice responses and attentiveness.

INCREASED LAY INVOLVEMENT

Involvement of lay members helps accomplish goals such as affirming the dignity of individuals, improving feelings of self-worth, increasing opportunities for self-expression, teaching about worship, and encouraging the responsiveness and attentiveness of the congregation. Worship leaders need to examine their attitudes toward lay participation. If participation of the laity is unwelcome in worship, does this communicate that serious participation is also unwelcome in other areas of congregational life?

Lay persons can be involved directly during worship in many ways. For example, congregation members may be included in speaking with unison Scripture reading, corporate response to the presentation of the offering, unison call to worship, unison benediction, responsive prayer, litany of thanksgiving, responsive call to worship, or unison statement of faith. Worshipers may be included in singing with hymns, musical call to worship, singing the Lord's Prayer, musical response to presentation of the offering, choirs and small ensembles, or a corporate musical benediction.

The worship committee can enable more frequent and in-depth lay leadership and participation in worship. Ceremonies and brief services can be developed that allow new traditions to become established that encourage adults and children to express their responses to God. The worship committee may schedule times when lay people, including the children's worship team, lead the congregation in worship songs and in prayer.

GIFTS AND TALENTS SURVEY

Each year, the worship committee may survey the congregation to discover gifts and talents available for worship services. Be sure to include children in this survey. The committee may find children who play musical instruments that would be good contributions to a worship service, such as guitars, harps, pianos, and instruments they play in school bands. Some children might learn to play tambourines and rhythm sticks. Other children might want to contribute dramatic presentations or Scripture readings or be ushers and greeters. Plan specific schedules for how children will be included.

POSSIBILITIES FOR WORSHIP

The following is an example of one church's brainstorm list for one month.

Week 1: A small group will read a passage of Scripture in several languages that represent members of the congregation. Use wind chimes, candles, mobiles, and windmills for a story about Pentecost.

Week 2: The children gather around the communion table for a prayer of blessing. Include a story about the meaning of communion.

Week 3: Members of the youth group act as greeters. A chancel drama is presented with someone dressed in old-fashioned clothes telling a story about the "olden days" of the church.

Week 4: Feature a dramatic interpretation of the call of Moses. Have a church member share a personal story about an area of ministry and how the person felt called to that ministry.

CHILDREN'S EDUCATIONAL PROGRAMS

Christian education activities might be used to prepare children to participate in congregational worship or to assist with leading congregational worship.

WORSHIP RELATED TO EDUCATION

Children will *experience* worship only through worship. Children will *learn about* worship through other experiences with the church's Christian education program. They can develop concepts about worship through experiences in Sunday school classes, in opening exercises for the entire membership of the Sunday school, in the nursery for infants and toddlers, and in youth programs.

COMPONENTS OF EDUCATION FOR WORSHIP

Education for worship should include opportunities to meet pastors and worship leaders; to explore the sanctuary to see the chancel, nave, pulpit, communion table, baptismal font or baptistry; to pass the offering plate; to follow the order of worship in the bulletin; to learn to use the hymnal and Bible; to sign the attendance form; and to pray the Lord's Prayer and recite the creeds. Children may learn the meanings of key words, such as *anthem, response, invocation, adoration, communion, Lord's Supper* or *Eucharist,* and *call to worship.*

RESOURCES FOR EDUCATION ABOUT WORSHIP

Many resources are available to assist Christian educators as they help children *learn about* worship. Some of these resources are listed here:

Alleluia Series, Augsburg Fortress, Publishers, 426 S. Fifth Street, Box 1209, Minneapolis, MN 55440, 1981. Sets of resources for children ages three years through senior high school provide opportunities for creative growth and a deeper understanding of traditional worship practices. Each year is coordinated with the three-year lectionary and includes 30 lessons.

Avery, Richard and Donald Marsh. *The Avery and Marsh Songbook.* Port Jarvis, NY: Proclamation Productions, Inc., 1972. Songs for congregations, choirs, groups, and soloists that encourage thoughtful participation in worship by young and old.

Christopher, Rachel and Huw. *Introduction to Worship.* Little Chapel on the Boardwalk, Box 4906, North Lumina Avenue and Oxford Street, Wrightsville Beach, NC 28480, 1986. A curriculum to introduce young elementary-age children and their parents to the elements of worship. Includes material about the church seasons, prayer (including the doxology and the Lord's Prayer), communion, and baptism.

Parish Teacher (Monthly). Augsburg Fortress, Publishers, 426 S. Fifth Street, Box 1209, Minneapolis, MN 55440. Offers creative ideas, helpful articles, new techniques for teachers of preschool through adult. Worship ideas often included.

Room to Grow. Augsburg Fortress, Publishers, 426 S. Fifth Street, Box 1209, Minneapolis, MN 55440, 1988. Resources for children ages three through seven years that help young children learn about their world and their relationship with God and with other people. Over 225 teaching experiences, including worship.

Schreivogel, Paul A. *Small Prayers for Small Children about Big and Little Things* and *More Prayers for Small Children.* Minneapolis, MN: Augsburg, 1980. A series of prayers for young children that help youngsters learn about prayer and that can help adults add insight and depth to their prayers. The prayers include talking and seeing in order to encourage active involvement in prayer by young children.

Smith, Judy Gattis. *Celebrating Special Days in the Church School Year: Liturgies and Participation Activities for Church School Children.* Colorado Springs, CO: Meriwether Publishing, Ltd., Publisher, 1981. Resources for adding involvement and inclusiveness to worship. Many ideas may be adapted for congregational worship.

Williams, Doris and Patricia Griggs. *Preparing for the Messiah: Ideas for Teaching/Celebrating Advent.* Nashville, TN: Abingdon Press, 1982. Practical and creative resources for church teachers, worship leaders, and families may be used in many situations. Includes hundreds of ideas and variations that build on traditions and create new customs. Many experiences may be adapted for other subjects and themes.

4 ADULT EDUCATION PROGRAMS

Adults can develop attitudes that anticipate growth and learning and that see other people, especially children, as individuals who can worship. To encourage adults to consider such attitudes, the worship committee can provide communication within the congregation in order to encourage full participation in worship.

The worship committee might write a series of newsletter articles. The series may explain how and why children are involved in worship and emphasize that worship is participation rather than performance. Newsletter articles might also give adults advance notice of the worship themes and music so they can review them with their children at home. A brochure for adults who do not have young children might encourage them to welcome young children who sit near them. The newsletter or the worship bulletins could describe a color, symbol, or key word for the worship service.

As the worship committee provides training for children and other lay persons who will be assisting with worship leadership responsibilities, the congregation may begin to celebrate diversity in worship. Adult education sessions can help reach this goal.

ADULT EDUCATION SESSIONS

Adults can be helped to understand child development, faith development, and appropriate responses to individual children. The worship committee or other groups might study relevant materials, such as *Will Our Children Have Faith?* by John H. Westerhoff III (1983) or *The Ministry of the Child* by Dennis C. Benson and Stan J. Stewart (1978).

For some adults, education for worship and including children in worship might happen through an adult education course or a retreat. The themes for a four-session course could include the meaning of worship, the development of the young child,

stages of faith development, and responding with children in worship.

SESSION 1: THE MEANING OF WORSHIP
OBJECTIVES
1. To define our individual understanding of worship
2. To learn the meaning of worship, for adults and for children
3. To participate in the creation of a small group worship experience

LEADER BACKGROUND
As mentioned earlier in this book, *worship* is derived from the Anglo-Saxon *weorthscipe* or "worthy ship." To the Christian, worship is a reverent response in thought, word, and deed to the supreme value of God's gift of Christ. Worship is central to our Christian faith. Worship is not for us, the people, but it is our service directed toward God through the words and actions of adoration, confession, thanksgiving, and commitment.

Worship is composed of individual acts, usually combined in a group experience, in which we respond to God as revealed to us in the life, death, and resurrection of Jesus Christ and in which we recognize God as holy, loving, and present with us. The essence of worship does not change with the age of the individual.

Can children worship? Children worship with each new discovery of their lives: stars, puppies, snowflakes. Reverence, adoration, respect, love, awe, praise, adoration, appreciation, and honor come naturally to children. Jesus himself valued their songs of praise during his final week on earth (Matthew 21:16).

The work of Sofia Cavalletti, author of *The Religious Potential of the Child*, was summarized in chapter 2. She believes that all children experience God, whether or not they are involved in organized religious education. She has seen a spiritual inclination in each child with whom she has worked and noticed that children showed their experiences with God. These experiences were characterized by their deep concentration and their spontaneous joy. Cavalletti maintains that young children are not just getting ready to learn about God, but that they can actually know, love, and worship God in ways that are appropriate for their understanding. She emphasizes that children are not just learning about God through explanation and interpretation, but they are actually worshiping by entering into the experience of the presence of God. The children are participating and "taking in" the experience (Cavalletti, 1982).

LEARNING ACTIVITIES

Lead the participants in some or all of these experiences. Select the learning activities that are appropriate for the adults in your particular group.

1. Present the above leader background material as a minilecture or as a handout. Multiple copies must include the name of this book, the author and publisher, and the phrase, "Used by permission."

2. Include discussion questions, such as:
   a. Sentence completion:
      "Worship is . . ."
      "For adults, worship is . . ."
      "For children, worship is . . ."
   b. How do you see God or think of God as you worship?
   c. What have you learned about God through worship?
   d. What have you learned about yourself through worship?
   e. How would you tell God that you love God?
   f. When do you feel closest to God?
   g. How do you think God feels about your worship?
   h. What would be different without worship?

3. Describe your most memorable worship experience.

4. Study the Bible on worship: Isaiah 6:1-8; Jeremiah 1:4-10; Luke 24:13-35; John 20:24-29. Consider: What happens in worship? What are the benefits of worship? What does worship say about us? What does worship say about God?

5. Examine the parts of the worship service, noting the sequence, as given in a worship bulletin or a denominational book of worship. Consider: What happens in worship? What are the benefits of worship? What does worship say about us? What does worship say about God?

6. Continue to think about the parts of a worship service using a worship bulletin or a denominational book of worship. Circle the parts that include music. Box the parts that include prayer. Underline the parts that include Scripture. Shade the parts that include the people addressing God. What does this say about worship and about God?

7. Review the seasons of the church year. See material included in chapter 5 of this book. Discuss how the seasons help us keep the stories of Jesus' life alive in worship.

8. Use group discussion to generate a "worship wheel" to illustrate worship. The "worship wheel" uses the idea of a "mindmap" to organize ideas and discover patterns that emerge during brainstorms. Use colored markers and newsprint. Write the main concept, worship, in the middle of the paper and draw a circle around it. Each time the group thinks of a new idea about worship draw a spoke out from the center, like the spokes of a wheel, and write the new idea at the end of the line. New ideas may naturally group themselves together, so you can draw smaller branches off the main spokes to show new associations. The same word or words may appear several times, which indicates their importance to this group and their connections with each other. Here is an example of the beginning of a "worship wheel" from one group:

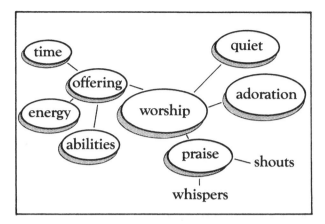

SESSION 2: THE DEVELOPMENT OF THE YOUNG CHILD

OBJECTIVES

1. To learn about the stages of cognitive, moral, and emotional development in children from birth to eight years of age
2. To reflect on our early worship memories
3. To consider possible congregational worship experiences that take into account the stages of child development

LEADER BACKGROUND

Many kinds of growth and development happen at the same time for young children. We cannot really separate one kind of development from another. A child is greater than the sum of the parts. All the parts are needed, although they may develop at different speeds. All the parts affect one another. Children learn best by participating actively rather than by passively watching or listening.

Learning happens best at very young ages, between birth and the age of five. And very young children learn best through their senses. The sounds, lights, colors, movement, and interaction of worship have great impact on young children, even more so if they are encouraged to participate.

COGNITIVE DEVELOPMENT

Although children can develop a sense of God's presence, their actual understanding of God cannot develop faster than their thinking ability. For young children, learning to think happens through internalizing patterns of behavior. Through the actions and words of worship, worship becomes part of a child's intellectual process. Sometimes adults will argue, "Children cannot participate because they do not yet understand." Other adults note that faith is caught rather than taught and that understanding will come later. Meaning is constructed by the child through experiences and by making connections about relationships.

Birth to two years: Children are egocentric and, therefore, think of themselves as the centers of the universe. Youngsters have difficulty in seeing things from the perspective of another person. The child assumes that his/her perception of objects and events is shared by everyone else. This means, for instance, that infants think objects exist only when they look directly at them. Children learn through their senses and physical movements.

Three to five years: Children are still egocentric, but they have moments of insight into the perspectives of others. They are able to role-play other perspectives in dramatic play. Concepts of space and time are limited to the child's personal experience. Children learn about cause and effect.

Six to eight years: Children begin to use mental images and language to symbolize the present and the real. However, children focus on one characteristic of an object or situation at a time. Therefore, the same amount of water in a short cup and in a tall cup looks like different amounts of water to them. Children are not able to think of both height and volume at the same time. Also, children can sort objects by one category, such as size or color, but not two or more categories, such as both size and color.

MORAL DEVELOPMENT

Characteristics of children have an impact on the ways in which they experience and learn about worship. If they feel good about themselves, they will feel that they are good and worthwhile in God's eyes.

Birth to two years: Because very young children are egocentric, they have difficulty imagining the feelings and responses of others. Children know right and wrong only by the reactions of adults who are present. They will or will not perform an action because the consequences might be pleasant or might be painful. Around age two years, youngsters seem to be internalizing the "rules," as illustrated by the way in which they say "no, no, no" to themselves as they try to play with a forbidden object. Internalizing rules comes with language.

Three to five years: At this age children may obey unquestioningly because of external rules. Being right is following the rules, just "because." The significance of disobedience is based on the magnitude of the observable consequences rather than on intentions. So, for example, breaking four glasses while trying to help is worse than breaking one glass while stealing cookies, because breaking four glasses is worse than breaking one.

Six to eight years: Children begin to develop a concept that what is right is whatever satisfies one's own needs: "I'll scratch your back if you scratch mine." In addition, children in this age group would likely approve of behavior that pleases significant adults.

EMOTIONAL DEVELOPMENT

Healthy emotional development will cause children to have an openness to themselves and to other people.

When all senses are involved in worship, children experience positive emotions. They want to learn more in order to become more involved. They are motivated to worship in ways they understand.

Birth to two years: Infants and toddlers need to develop a basic trust in themselves, significant people, objects, and events. An infant's trust becomes a mixture of faith and realism in an older person. Toddlers begin to develop a sense of self and autonomy, rather than shame and self-doubt. They need opportunities to be independent and develop self-esteem. Children are developing a valuable sense of dignity and personhood.

Three to five years: Youngsters seek to develop a sense of initiative, rather than guilt. Children need opportunities to explore, to choose, to plan, to act. They are learning how to set goals and try to achieve them. They learn that they can make things happen.

Six to eight years: School-age children are developing skills for accomplishing tasks. They develop a sense of industry, rather than inferiority, as they learn to enjoy the pleasure of completing work through attention and perseverance.

LEARNING ACTIVITIES

Lead the participants in some or all of these experiences. Select the learning activities that are appropriate for the adults in your particular group.

1. Present the above leader background material as a minilecture or as a handout. Multiple copies must include the name of this book, the author and publisher, and the phrase, "Used by permission."
2. Include discussion questions, such as:
   a. What does the study of child development indicate about how children best learn?
   b. Describe which aspects of a child's development make it possible for children to develop faith.
   c. How can adults foster children's awareness of wonder and awe?
   d. How might the parent-child relationship affect the child's concepts of God?
3. Brainstorm lists of characteristics of children at each age level.
4. List ways in which children learn. Erickson (1963) defined the following stages of psychosocial development:
   a. trust (from hugs and encouragement; when their needs for food, warmth, and love are met; repeated experiences with loving church people)
   b. autonomy (from being loved even when they rebel; experiencing clear and consistent limits; being allowed to maintain their personal dignity)
   c. initiative (when attempts are welcomed; questions are answered; experiencing some freedom of choice; being allowed to accept responsibility)
   d. industry (children are allowed to follow through; adults value children for themselves; children are led to consider reasons and motives for behavior)
5. List religious ideas, beliefs, and concepts you had as a child.

6. Discuss the earliest prayer you remember.

7. Using chapter 5 of this book, the adult education leader might select a worship activity that would address each stage of cognitive, moral, and emotional development. Include the adult education group in planning and carrying out these worship activities.

SESSION 3: THE STAGES OF FAITH DEVELOPMENT

OBJECTIVES

1. To define individual understandings of faith
2. To learn the stages of faith development
3. To consider possible congregational worship experiences to facilitate the faith development of young children

LEADER BACKGROUND

Persons who worship together are often at various stages of faith development. John H. Westerhoff III (1976) has suggested a simple model to describe the meaning of faith at various age levels. If faith is "caught, not taught," then worship is a place to experience growth and change in the faith development process. Individuals in each stage contribute to the general health of the congregation.

The first stage of *experienced faith* occurs during the early childhood years. Youngsters explore and test, imagine and create, observe and copy, experience and react. Faith is experienced by action. For young children, the words that are spoken do not matter as much as the experiences they have that relate to the words. They need to experience trust, love, and acceptance. Children will experience the meaning of adult faith words as they experience the actions from adults that fulfill those words.

By including young children in worship, the worship community will observe the characteristics of young children and young children will experience the meaning of inclusion in the faith. The congregation can offer

1. a warm, welcoming, inviting, and positive atmosphere.
2. feelings, memories, concepts, words, and symbols of the faith experience, with which

the children later will construct their own faith.
3. adults who are trustworthy, accepting, and affirming.

In the later stage of *affiliative faith,* the faith of the child is based on the models of parents and other adults. The child wants to identify and stand with the faith of the persons who are important in his or her life. Youngsters have a natural ability to wonder, question, create, imagine, and initiate. Children want to learn the rituals and patterns of the worshiping community. They store up their impressions of awe and wonder for God before they even know the meanings of the words we use about God. The priorities of young children are based on the priorities of those whom the children trust.

Children cannot find a place in the faith community if they are kept on the fringes of experience. Adults should seek to bring their children near the traditions of their faith. By including children in worship, the congregation's experience can be that of involvement and participation. The congregation can offer

1. opportunities for children to become "beginners" in the faith, through dedication or baptism, receiving Bibles, learning words such as *worship, prayer, pastor, pulpit.*
2. opportunities for children to contribute their own gifts to worship experiences, to be the "actors" and to respond to God as their audience.
3. adults who are trustworthy, accepting, and affirming.

Children learn and worship best in concrete ways and by using all senses. God seems to have designed the whole human race with that in the plan—even adults! He revealed himself to the Hebrews with pillars of cloud and fire and rations of manna. He sent Jesus Christ to be God with us— to be seen by us and to speak to us and to touch us. In baptism and the Lord's Supper, we have been given concrete symbols of how Jesus is accessible to every person. Developing more concrete forms for worship that include children will result in enrichment for everyone.

During the stage of *searching faith,* the adolescent reacts to the values that were unquestioningly accepted earlier. The teenager looks for new rituals, forms, and styles to express all areas of life, including faith and worship. Young people challenge the church with their insights and innovations. By questioning the inherited values, adolescents develop ownership of the faith that surrounded them in their early years. Youths construct a faith system from the priorities that are most relevant to their lives.

Youths form their own memories and personalize their own faith. By including adolescents in worship, the worship experience will be relevant and responsive to the concerns of the world around us. The congregation can offer

1. opportunities to express feelings.
2. rich worship experiences.
3. models of worship language and feelings.
4. people who are willing to listen and respond to questions.
5. celebrations from which to draw memories.

At *mature faith* (sometimes called owned faith), individuals integrate experiences of earlier stages. Mature faith is flexible and open and reflects a personal relationship with God based on freedom rather than on authority. Adults seek to combine the inherited faith with their personal faith as a foundation for the future. Persons at this stage seek to share their perspective with those in earlier stages. Adults bring a sense of meaning, continuity, and challenge to the experience of worship.

LEARNING ACTIVITIES

Lead the participants in some or all of these experiences. Select the learning activities that are appropriate for the adults in your particular group.

1. Present the above leader background material as a minilecture or as a handout. Multiple copies must include the name of this book, the author and publisher, and the phrase, "Used by permission."
2. Include discussion questions, such as:
   a. What makes my life complete? What makes my life meaningful?
   b. Where do I ultimately place my trust?
   c. Describe your earliest memory of worship. At what stage of faith development were you? Why did that memory stay with you?
   d. What is the relationship between the faith of the parents and the faith of their children?
   e. How do children develop a concept of God and of relating to God?
   f. How are parents encouraging or inhibiting their children's faith development?
3. View the film, *The Mouths of Babes,* Tom Christensen (1984). Available from: Mass Media Ministries, 2116 North Charles Street, Baltimore, MD 21218, and Augsburg Fortress, Audiovisual Department, 426 South Fifth Street, Box 1209, Minneapolis, MN 55440.
4. List characteristics you would want to see in persons of mature faith. Discuss how those qualities and values are developed.
5. Identify characteristics of worship. Select a hymn to express each characteristic. Select a children's song to express each characteristic.
6. List ways we can communicate about worship with young children.
7. Examine an order of worship from a worship bulletin or a denominational worship book. Make notes about which senses are used at each point during the service. Use information from elsewhere in this book as a resource. Are all senses used at one time or another?

SESSION 4: RESPONDING WITH CHILDREN IN WORSHIP

OBJECTIVES

1. To examine similarities and differences in how adults and children respond to God.
2. To define ways to help children worship God.
3. To consider ways to include children in congregational worship.

LEADER BACKGROUND

Because of their different levels of development, children at different ages will perceive worship experiences, such as the Sacrament of Holy Baptism, differently.

In many denominations, infants and toddlers are likely to be those being baptized in a service of baptism. Their perception is strictly sensorimotor: they feel held in the arms of a stranger; they are tipped off balance; their head is wet; they hear strange voices. Without language and prior experience, they do not understand the meaning of the event and can only have feelings about the event.

Children between three and five years of age can learn that baptism is something that involves water, people, special clothing, and the pastor in front of the congregation. They see a child being held; they hear water splashing; they see people shaking hands and perhaps hugging. They may have had prior experience with water for washing, drinking, and watering plants, but the few drops involved in some infant baptisms may not seem like enough to accomplish anything to youngsters in this age group. They do not yet have enough symbolic language to connect the experience with the meaning of the event.

Young children between six and eight years also become aware that baptism is something that involves water, people, special clothing, and the pastor in front of the congregation. Now, though, they are aware of the presence of the baptismal font. They begin to feel included or excluded in the experience. Children in this age group need opportunities to observe baptisms closely; to experience water in bathing, swimming, walking in the rain; to visit the baptismal font and touch the water; to learn to say, spell, and write the word "baptism"; and to hear stories and see photos and the certificate of their own baptism.

LEARNING ACTIVITIES

Lead the participants in some or all of these experiences. Select the learning activities that are appropriate for the adults in your particular group.

1. Present the above leader background material as a minilecture or as a handout. Multiple copies must include the name of this book, the author and publisher, and the phrase, "Used by permission."
2. Include discussion questions, such as:
   a. What do you remember about worship?
   b. What do you appreciate most about worship?
   c. What is the mood of your congregation in worship?
   d. What is the meaning of your congregation's worship for children between birth and two years old? between three and five years old? between six and eight years old?
   e. What does it mean to be part of "the family of God"?
   f. What worship activities would you use with children and why?
   g. What would you like to change about the ways in which your congregation worships?
3. Complete this sentence: "God shows up in unexpected ways, such as . . ."
4. Divide into groups of up to six people, but be sure to have at least three small groups. Have each group consider your congregation's worship service from only one point of view: a) through the eyes of the worship leader, b) through the eyes of God, c) through the eyes of a child. If your group is large, more than one small group can deal with each perspective. Respond to these questions:
   a. What insights do you get from looking at the worship service through someone else's eyes?
   b. How is your perspective of worship different from the perspectives of others?
5. Brainstorm ways to help children participate in congregational worship in your church.
6. Using chapter 5 of this book, the adult eduation leader might select a worship activity that would address each stage of cognitive, moral, and emotional development. Include the adult education group in planning and carrying out these worship activities.

CONCLUSION

Those who plan and guide worship should lead so simply that people look beyond them to see and respond to God. When worship is oriented solely around intellectual communications, some of the adult congregation, as well as children, will feel left out. To be complete, worship should include our emotions as well as our intellect. Worship should really involve the worshipers in participation.

When services incorporate elements of worship that most people can understand and in which they can participate, children will naturally be involved in offering praise to God.

5 Ways to Include Children in Worship

There are many ideas that worship committees can use in assisting their churches in welcoming children into congregational worship. In the rest of this chapter, you will find ideas for brochures and bulletins; approaches to prayer, music, and drama; the Lord's Supper; sermon guidelines; using Scripture; and incorporating the creative arts. The intent of these activities is to encourage the participation of children, youth, and adults in the community worship experience, but some of these activities will also be useful for Christian education programming.

"God calls for worship that involves our whole being. The body, mind, spirit, and emotions should all be laid on the altar of worship. Often we have forgotten that worship should include the body as well as the mind and spirit" (Foster 1978, 147).

Our whole being involves a lot! When we get totally involved, we are using more than just the five senses. We could say we are using eleven senses, and there may even be more.

1. vision, our eyesight, with which we perceive physical characteristics, colors, shapes, sizes, and much more.
2. hearing, which allows us to be aware of sounds.
3. touch, which enables us to physically feel objects.
4. taste, with which we sense flavors.
5. smell, which enables us to sense odors.
6. kinesthetic sense, which tells us when parts of our bodies or muscles are tense, relaxed, in motion or at rest.
7. visceral sense, which is our instinctive and intuitive behavior.
8. balance, our sense of equilibrium or steadiness.
9. spatial sense, with which we understand the expanse of our environment and the distance of other objects.
10. sense of time, with which we become aware of the duration that something lasts.
11. spiritual, with which we get in touch with the nonphysical or spiritual world.

Using all our senses in worship enriches our participation in worship. When our senses are totally involved:

1. the meaning of worship is enhanced. We more fully experience God's presence.
2. we are following scriptural examples of worship. The setting is seen through our vision; the music employs our hearing; flowers and lighted candles exercise our sense of smell; hands shaken in greeting involve touch and movement; and the Lord's Supper involves taste, smell, and touch.
3. we actively participate in the celebration.
4. worship becomes memorable as we are sometimes taken unaware.

Worship planners and leaders can design services to incorporate the senses meaningfully. Be sure that there is meaning behind the experiences included in worship services. Avoid the staged theatrics of artificial and unusual events included just to be different or entertaining. Be sensitive to the mood and feelings of the congregation. Refrain from incorporating extremely unusual experiences too frequently. Incorporate experiences that have substance rather than those that are showy.

BROCHURES AND BULLETINS

Three items are described in this section. The first is a brochure called "Making Room for Children in Worship," which presents the congregation's attitudes about worship and includes suggestions for adults on ways they can assist children who are worshiping with them. The second is bulletin covers that use children's artwork. These help youngsters realize that their gifts are of value and feel included in the congregation's experiences. The third is a children's worship activity bulletin that helps children follow along with the service in a form and with words that they can understand.

Making Room for Children in Worship

A guide for parents and friends of children who come to worship with us.

Church Name
Street Address
City, State, Zip Code
Telephone Number

● "MAKING ROOM FOR CHILDREN IN WORSHIP" BROCHURE

The worship brochure described here, "Making Room for Children in Worship," explains to parents and other worshipers why and how children are welcome in the worshiping community. The worship committee will want to adapt this material to fit the traditions of its specific congregation.

Ages: readers.

Source: Adapted from material from several churches.

Children at Worship

WELCOME to worship at _____ Church! As you look around the sanctuary, you will see that children are part of our worshiping community. Their presence here grows out of the biblical tradition and conviction that children are members of the covenant community.

We make room for children in our worship by:
● scheduling children's worship festivals, which engage children in a variety of ways throughout the year.
● making sure that worship activity bulletins and Bible story books are available for younger children in worship.

This folder was designed to aid parents and other members of our congregation in making room for children at worship. Our Board of Christian Education hopes you will read its contents.

The Prekindergarten Child

Parents may wonder at the wisdom of including prekindergarten children in worship. Children may be restless, distracting those around them and embarrassing their parents with their behavior.

The young child comes to worship with:
● a rather limited attention span.
● seemingly unlimited energy.
● a growing curiosity about everything.

While these ingredients can combine to test the patience of adults, there are several things parents can do to make the child's experience—and their own—more relaxed and worshipful:
● sit near the front where your child can clearly see the chancel.
● prepare your child for the different parts of the worship service; explain special events ahead of time and answer questions that need an answer right now in a quiet whisper.
● encourage use of the children's worship activity bulletin, available from the ushers, and invite your child to color or draw in those bulletins.
● allow your child to bring a favorite stuffed animal along or pick up a Bible story book in the library to browse.

A sensitivity to the young child's abilities and needs can help make worship a more pleasant and meaningful experience for everyone.

The School-Age Child

The school-age child brings some new abilities to worship:

- a greater capacity for attentive listening.
- an increasing ability to read.
- the ability to organize and memorize information.

Parents can help their school-age child toward greater participation in worship as these capacities develop:

- use a version of Scripture in contemporary English language.
- help in reading or memorizing of the Lord's Prayer, the Apostles' Creed, and other parts of the worship service.
- review the bulletin with your child to identify new or difficult words and preview together those parts when the congregation responds by reading and speaking.
- invite your child to follow the reading of the Scripture lesson in the Bible.
- find hymns and go over the words.
- encourage your child to listen to the sermon for stories, answers to questions, or important thoughts.

For this age group, some parts of the children's worship activity bulletins will be more meaningful because of the child's ability to read. The regular worship bulletin will also be useful.

Worship and Learning

Worship is God-centered praise and adoration. The church's worship service is also one basic way by which people learn what it means to be Christian. Children learn worship by worshiping with the congregation Sunday after Sunday.

- They learn they belong to Christ and are welcome in Christ's church.
- They come to know the Lord's Prayer, the Apostles' Creed, and other parts of the service from memory.
- They build a fund of memorable, shared experiences of Christian community from which they may draw when they are older.

- They are enriched by the beauty of music and art as expressions of praise and as human responses to God.
- They hear stories from the Bible read and interpreted; and they begin to see Christian worship as one place where God may speak to them.
- They witness the drama of baptism and communion as signs of God's kindness and favor.
- They discover that they are valued as persons by God and by God's people at church.

Bringing children to worship may not always be easy, but it is an essential part of their growth toward Christ.

ABCs for Parents and Friends of Children

Arrive in time to find a good place to sit. Sit near the front to provide younger children with a better view of the chancel. Children's Bible story books are placed in pew racks in the first three rows.

Bring colored pencils or crayons for children to use as they draw in the children's worship activity bulletins. Ushers will be happy to give your child one of the children's worship activity bulletins when you are seated.

Clue your child about what will happen next in worship. Children who can read will want to find the hymns. They like to be ready.

In the home, discuss worship to prepare children for any change in the routine, such as a baptism or other special features. Also, take time to answer questions about worship experiences.

Express your gladness at having children in worship. After the service, be sure to welcome the children near you. Include them in your conversations to let them know they belong.

Free yourself from worry about children's behavior. Be open to receiving their ministry to you.

● BULLETIN COVERS DESIGNED BY CHILDREN

Children's artwork can be used as the basis for the cover design of worship bulletins.

THANKSGIVING

Children use dark magic markers to draw pictures related to the theme. They can use 8½″ x 11″ white paper if the church has a copy machine that reduces the size of the drawings to fit the cover of the worship bulletin. Otherwise use paper the size of the bulletin cover itself. Identify the artist on the bulletin cover or inside the bulletin.

VARIATIONS

1. Children produce their drawings as the culmination of a unit of study in Sunday school or choir.

2. Use a single drawing and duplicate it for all covers.
3. Use a combination of small designs and duplicate the composite for all covers.
4. Have children decorate covers individually so each member of the congregation has a unique bulletin cover design.

Possible themes: Thanksgiving, Advent, Christmas, Epiphany, Bible stories.

Source: First Covenant Church, St. Paul, Minnesota.

● CHILDREN'S WORSHIP ACTIVITY BULLETINS

In children's worship activity bulletins, the parts of the worship service are translated into a form and words that young children more easily understand.

Words for the hymns are written stanza by stanza, because young children have difficulty following in the hymnal when the lines of words are divided by lines of music. Words to the Lord's Prayer, the Apostles' Creed, and other parts of the service are included in the bulletin. Some explanation about the history of the hymns or the Scripture can be included. An activity sheet is added that relates to the theme of the worship service. Identify the writer(s) and illustrator(s) on the bulletin cover or inside.

Ages: four years and up.

VARIATIONS:

1. Have children develop illustrations for the children's activity bulletin cover.
2. Include announcements of coming events that are of interest to children and families.
3. Add a checklist of things to look for in the upcoming worship service: Scripture lessons, symbols, themes, leaders, music.
4. Include definitions of key terms and difficult words that are used in the Bible readings or the sermon.
5. Add an interview with a church staff member or volunteer church teacher.
6. Write background information about worship leaders.
7. Include the text of the choir anthems.
8. Leave space to write prayers or draw pictures related to the worship theme.
9. Provide crayons with the worship activity bulletin.
10. Provide book markers for children to mark the correct places in their Bibles and hymnals.
11. Explain about symbols in colors, music, architecture, and seasons of the church year.
12. Add directions for a family devotional activity.
13. Include puzzles as well as pencil and paper games related to the theme.
14. Include directions asking children to circle all parts of worship service that are musical, box all parts that are prayer, underline all parts that include Scripture, and shade in the parts that the congregation does.

Source: Crosstown Covenant Church, Minneapolis, Minnesota. Sources for material for children's worship activity sheets: Abingdon Press, 201–8th Ave. So., Nashville, TN 37202. Shining Star, Good Apple, Inc., Box 299, Carthage, IL 62321-0299.

On the following pages is an example of a Children's Worship Activity Bulletin

CHILDREN'S BULLETIN
SUNDAY MORNING WORSHIP

Pre-Service Hymn Sing

Organ Prelude (Music played by handbells and organ to help us get ready to worship.)

Welcome and Announcements
Wednesday 7:00 Children's Bible classes and singing
Next Sunday 12:00 All-church picnic

Hymn   *"This Is My Father's World"*

1. *This is my Father's world, and to my listening ears*
   All nature sings, and round me rings the music of the spheres.
   This is my Father's world; I rest me in the thought
   Of rocks and trees, of skies and seas;
   His hand the wonders wrought.

2. *This is my Father's world; the birds their carols raise;*
   The morning light, the lily white, declare their maker's praise.
   This is my Father's world; he shines in all that's fair.
   In the rustling grass I hear him pass;
   He speaks to me everywhere.

3. *This is my Father's world; Oh, let me not forget*
   That, though the wrong seems oft so strong, God is the ruler yet.
   This is my Father's world; why should my heart be sad?
   The Lord is king, let the heavens ring;
   God reigns, let the earth be glad!

   Lutheran Book of Worship 554

Opening Prayer

(The worship leader will offer a prayer to ask God to be present during worship.)

The Lord's Prayer

Our Father, who art in heaven, hallowed be thy name. Thy kingdom come. Thy will be done on earth as it is in heaven. Give us this day our daily bread. And forgive us our sins, as we forgive those who sin against us. And lead us not into temptation, but deliver us from evil. For thine is the kingdom and the power and the glory forever and ever. Amen.

Ministry of Music

(Our organist and her sisters will be singing this morning.)

Congregational Prayer

Offering

(You may put your offering in the offering plate as it is passed to you.)

Hymn   *"Blest Be the Tie that Binds"*

1. *Blest be the tie that binds*
   Our hearts in Christian love;
   The unity of heart and mind
   Is like to that above.

2. *Before our Father's throne*
   We pour our ardent prayers;
   Our fears, our hopes, our aims are one,
   Our comforts and our cares.

3. *We share our mutual woes,*
   Our mutual burdens bear,
   And often for each other flows
   The sympathizing tear.

4. *From sorrow, toil, and pain,*
   And sin we shall be free;
   And perfect love and frienship reign
   Through all eternity.

Lutheran Book of Worship 370

Scripture Reading Ephesians 4:1-7, 11-16
(Look up the Scripture to read.)
Gospel Reading John 6:1-15
We remain standing with respect for God's Word in the Bible.

Message "We Need Each Other"

Hymn   *"Built on a Rock"*

1. *Built on a rock the Church shall stand,*
   Even when steeples are falling;
   Crumbled have spires in ev'ry land,
   Bells still chiming and calling—
   Calling the young and old to rest,
   Calling the souls of those distressed,
   Longing for life everlasting.

2. *Not in our temples made with hands*
   God, the Almighty, is dwelling;
   High in the heav'ns his temple stands,
   All earth temples excelling.
   Yet he who dwells in heav'n above
   Deigns to bide with us in love,
   Making our bodies his temple.

3. *We are God's house of living stones,*
   Built for his own habitation;
   He fills our hearts, his humble thrones,
   Granting us life and salvation.
   Were two or three to seek his face,
   He in their midst would show his grace,
   Blessings upon them bestowing.

4. *Yet in this house, an earthly frame,*
   Jesus the children is blessing;
   Hither we come to praise his name,
   Faith in our Savior confessing.
   Jesus to us his Spirit sent,
   Making with us his covenant,
   Granting his children the kingdom.

5. *Through all the passing years, O Lord,*
   Grant that, when church bells are ringing,
   Many may come to hear God's Word
   Where he this promise is bringing;
   I know my own, my own know me;
   You, not the world, my face shall see;
   My peace I leave with you. Amen.

Lutheran Book of Worship 365

Benediction

(The pastor will pray a prayer that recognizes that a blessing has been received from God.)

Organ Response

Postlude   "Jubilate Deo"

Did You Know . . . ?

Paul was in jail many times. He wrote his letter to the people who lived in a city called Ephesus while he was in jail.

When the Bible talks about being humble, it means we are not to think we are better than others but realize that God gives each of us many abilities.

In Ephesians 4:1-6 that Pastor Bill read, there were seven "ones." Take another look at those verses and see if you can find all of them.

PRAYER

Parents and Sunday school teachers can help children memorize the Lord's Prayer, the creeds, and the responses so they can join with the congregation.

Use prayers written by the children. When the worship leaders begin prayer with "boys and girls, women and men, let us pray . . .," everyone is included.

● THE LORD'S PRAYER

Here is a suggestion for children to lead the congregation in the Lord's Prayer with hand and body motions. They will need to learn the Lord's Prayer and practice the movements ahead of time.

Our Father, who art in heaven,

hallowed be thy name,

thy kingdom come,

thy will be done, on earth

as it is in heaven.	Give us this day our daily bread;
and forgive our sins,	as we forgive those who sin against us;
and lead us not into temptation,	but deliver us from evil.

| For thine is the kingdom, | and the power, and the glory, | forever and ever. Amen. |

Ages: four years and up.

Variations:

1. Several children can do these motions in the front of the church while someone sings the Lord's Prayer set to music.
2. Teach some of the movements to the congregation so everyone can participate in prayer motions.

Other possibilities: Bible verses such as John 3:16, Psalm 23; hymn stanzas.

Source: Victoria Wilson, First Covenant Church, St. Paul, Minnesota.

MUSIC

The children's choir is just one way to involve children in the music of worship. In addition, Sunday school groups may prepare illustrations or sign language presentations for hymns. Children or adults may prepare a liturgical dance to make visible the words or the feelings of music.

● ILLUSTRATED HYMNS

Children's artwork is used as the basis for illustrations on posters to accompany one of the hymns. Children stand in front of the church to hold up their illustrations during the appropriate line or stanza.

CAN YOU COUNT THE STARS?

1. Can you count the stars that bright-ly twink-le in __ the mid-night
2. Do you know how man-y midg-es in the noon-day sun play
3. Do you know how man-y chil-dren rise each morn-ing blithe and

sky? Can you count the clouds so light-ly o'er the
'round? Do you know how man-y fish-es in the
gay? Can you count their jol-ly voic-es sing-ing

mead-ows float-ing by? God the Lord__ doth mark their
cool-ing streams can be found? God the Lord__ called each of
sweet-ly day by day? God hears all __ their hap-py

num-ber with his eyes__ that nev-er slum-ber. He hath
them by name, and re-joic-ing in-to life they came. And he
voic-es in their pret-ty songs re-joic-es. And he

made them ev-'ry one. __ He hath made them ev-'ry one.
knows them ev-'ry one. __ And he knows them ev-'ry one.
loves them ev-'ry one. __ And he loves them ev-'ry one.

Text: Traditional
Music: Traditional;
  arr. Mary Tornquist

On 8½″ x 11″ or larger white paper, children can use dark magic markers to draw pictures related to the images in each line of the hymn. Use a copy machine or overhead projector that enlarges copy, enlarge the drawings to poster size. Children can paint or color the posters. Identify the artist(s) on the lower right corner.

Ages: four years and up.

Variations:

1. Children produce their drawings as the culmination of a unit of study in Sunday school or choir.
2. Children produce montages with magazine pictures that illustrate the subjects of each line of the hymn.
3. Use hymns with lots of imagery that draw on the experiences of children.
4. Use new hymns that children are just learning and would like to teach the congregation.
5. Children produce their drawings on write-on slides or blank filmstrip. Old, unwanted filmstrips may be cleaned with liquid bleach, rinsed in clear water, and dried to use again.

● SONG IN SIGN LANGUAGE

Sign language, the language of people who are hearing impaired, uses gestures and movement to communicate. Sign language may be used to interpret a hymn or anthem or to interpret a recited text. For young children, it may be a way to communicate physically—and to remember the song through the movements.

1. Select a well-known hymn or chorus so that the children's choir can concentrate on the sign language.
2. Select the signs for key words or phrases.
3. Practice the song and signs together.

Ages: six years and up.

Resources: Costello, Elaine. *Religious Signing: The New Comprehensive Guide for All Faiths.* New York, NY: Bantam Press, 1986.

Fant, Louie J. *Sign Language.* Acton, CA: Joyce Media, Inc., 1977.

Lane, Leonard G. *The Gallaudet Survival Guide to Signing.* Washington, D. C.: Gallaudet University Press, 1987.

O'Rourke, Terrence J. *A Basic Vocabulary: American Sign Language for Parents and Children.* Silver Spring, MD: T. J. Publishers, Inc., 1978.

Pentz, Croft M. and Carter E. Bearden. *Ministry to the Deaf.* New Wilmiongton, PA: House of Bon Giovanni, 1984.

Riekehof, Lottie L. *The Joy of Signing.* Springfield, MO: Gospel Publishing House, 1987.

Riekehof, Lottie L. *Talk to the Deaf.* Springfield, MO: Gospel Publishing House, 1963.

God   is   so good. (repeat 3 times)

God   is   good   to   me.

God   loves   me so. (repeat 3 times)

God   is   good   to   me.

Jesus   died   for   me. (repeat 3 times)

Jesus   is   good   to   me.

I   will do   God's will. (repeat 3 times)

God   is   good   to   me.

● LITURGICAL DANCE

> *"Praise the Lord. Sing to the Lord a new song, his praise in the assembly of the saints. . . . Let them praise his name with dancing and make music to him with tambourine and harp." Psalm 149:1, 3.*

Liturgical dance is worship in action—prayer in motion. Gestures and movement become a form of profound and wordless communication. Whether as a soloist or a small choir, whether young or old, each person in liturgical dance is interpreting worship as an individual with unique expressions, while still part of a whole.

Movements may be used to interpret a hymn or anthem or to interpret a recited text— always for the glory of God.

To prepare a liturgical dance:

1. Review the anthem or text. Play the music. Say the words out loud. Sing it over a period of several weeks at rehearsal.
2. Encourage the children or adults to express their feelings in movements. Feel the music. Feel the words. Watch which movements seem to be most natural for the children. Allow children or adults to use tambourines and hand clapping as appropriate.
3. Select the movements that the children or adults will use for key words or phrases. Choreograph these movements into a liturgical dance. Develop facial expressions, body movements, hand movements, and body postures.
4. Decide how to move around in the space available: chancel, aisles, steps.
5. Practice the dance for several weeks. Then use the liturgical dance during worship.

Ages: four years and up.

Variations:

1. Invite someone to tell the story about the writing of the anthem's words or tune.
2. Try simple rhythmic stepping.
3. Use instruments for a children's procession on All Saints' Day to the hymn, "For All the Saints," or some other festival with an appropriate hymn. Entire families could be included in the procession.
4. Have each child wear a white tunic to keep the focus on the group as a whole.
5. Attach colored ribbons or streamers to the tambourines for a celebration effect.

Resources:
Sacred Dance Guild of America.
Taylor, Margaret F. *A Time to Dance: Symbolic Movement in Worship.* Austin, TX: Sharing Co., 1980.
Source: Victoria Wilson, First Covenant Church, St. Paul, Minnesota.

Here are some suggested movements for a solo dancer to accompany the Magnificat (Mary's song, Luke 1:46-55). You may want to obtain a copy of the song "My Soul Doth Magnify the Lord," by Randall Thompson, which is based on Luke 1:46-55, translated from Latin, or use another version from a hymnal.

Introduction to be read:

> How do we express our joy? Smiles, tears, clapping, jumping, playing instruments, singing, dancing. The Bible tells us that all these have been used in the worship of God.

Many years ago, a young girl named Mary was very joyful. She would be the mother of Jesus, God's Son. Mary was so happy that she sang a wonderful song, called the "Magnificat." She praised God for all God had done and would do for the people.

Jesus was going to be born as a baby, in a human body. The Bible says that God became flesh. Jesus was God in a body. People would be able to see Jesus and hear Jesus and touch Jesus.

This morning, some friends are going to interpret Mary's wonderful song for us.

_____ will play the music on the piano. _____ will sing the words. _____ will interpret Mary's joy in movement. This is one way to give the words of Mary's song a body—to make it visible and audible and touchable.

The children are invited to the front of the sanctuary so they can see and hear.

1. Begin crouched near right side of chancel. Slowly rise and turn two times. Finish standing at center of chancel with arms stretched up.

2. Hands roll upwards, like joy bubbling out from inside the body.

"My soul glorifies the Lord,"

"and my spirit rejoices in God my Savior."

3. Descend chancel steps and finish near center aisle in a crouching position.

4. Stand. Bring arm half circle from waist out to right side. Bend arms at elbows with hands near ears, palms up. Drop arms to sides. Stand with confidence.

"For he has been mindful of the humble state of his servant."

"From now on all generations call me blessed,"

5. Move across nave to the left. Hold up a strong arm with fist. Move hand gently with open palm in to chest.

6. Stretch right arm out to side. Bring arm in to chest. Extend arm slowly and fully upwards, while ascending chancel steps.

"For the Mighty One has done great things for me—"

"holy is his name."

7. Touch right shoulder with right hand. Hands roll downward and outward while descending steps.

8. Raise strong arm with fist.

"His mercy extends to those who fear him, from generation to generation."

"He has performed mighty deeds with his arm;"

9. Circle hands at sides of heads.

10. Firmly swoop arms down to one side while descending to floor of nave.

"He has scattered those who are proud in their inmost thoughts."

"He has brought down rulers from their thrones"

11. Lift arms to other side while ascending two steps.

12. Lower hand from upper chest to abdomen. Gather arms to middle.

"but has lifted up the humble."

"He has filled the hungry with good things"

13. Open palms at chest. Push palms out and down.

14. Walk up steps with strong out firm steps, as if carrying a load. Stand at center of chancel. Raise hands upwards. Stand strong.

"but has sent the rich away empty."

"He has helped his servant Israel, remembering to be merciful"

15. Drop hand from chin outward. Lower hands from chin, as if stroking beard.

16. Cross right arm across waist in front. Cross left arm behind back. Rotate body to the right at least one full turn or more.

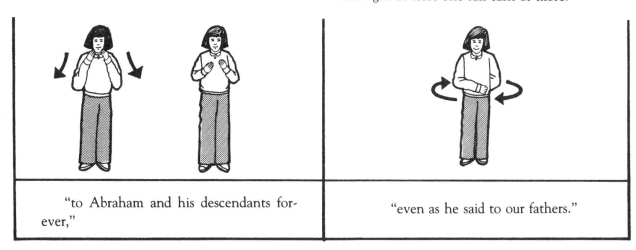

"to Abraham and his descendants forever,"

"even as he said to our fathers."

MUSICAL INSTRUMENTS

Music is important in the Bible. Many passages, even outside of the Psalms, were actually hymns and songs or choruses. Musical instruments are often referred to in the Bible. Psalm 150 refers to trumpet, harp, lyre, tambourine, strings, flute, and cymbals. An adapted version follows.

PSALM 150

Praise the Lord.
Praise God in God's sanctuary; praise God in God's mighty heavens.
Praise God for God's acts of power; praise God for God's surpassing greatness.
Praise God with the sounding of the trumpet; praise God with the harp and lyre,
praise God with tambourine and dancing; praise God with the strings and flute,
praise God with the clash of cymbals; praise God with resounding cymbals.
Let everything that has breath praise the Lord.
Praise the Lord.

Some instruments to make:
Dried beans in aluminum pie pans or paper plates (seal with staples or masking tape) to rattle.
Coffee can drums to beat.
Wooden blocks and rhythm sticks to hit together.
Clay flowerpots to tap.
Large rubber bands around a shoebox to pluck.
Bells to shake.
Ages: two years and up.

Variations:
1. Invite someone experienced with musical instruments to tell a Bible story (such as David and his harp, 1 Samuel 16:14-23) from one instrument's point of view.
2. Use kitchen utensils to create instruments and sounds.
3. Try simple rhythmic clapping.
4. Use instruments for a procession on All Saints' Day to the hymn, "For All the Saints," or for some other festival with an appropriate hymn. Entire families could be included in the procession.
Possible themes: Bible passages or hymns appropriate for Thanksgiving, Advent, Christmas, or Epiphany.
Source: Maricela Olvera, Cuautitlán Izcalli Covenant Church, Cuautitlán Izcalli, Mexico

DRAMA

Jesus Christ told stories that included much suspense, drama, and surprise. Scripture includes illustrations of the pageantry of worship. Drama in contemporary worship can accomplish many goals. Suggestions are presented here for processions; stories presented in drama, puppets, and shadow plays; and messages carried by Christian clowns, fools for Christ.

● PROCESSIONS

Processions add drama to many worship themes, from the celebrative, such as Palm Sunday, Easter, and Pentecost, to the more unusual, such as the exodus from Egypt, the taking of Jericho, going to Jerusalem for Passover, animals entering the ark, David's returning the Ark of the Covenant to Jerusalem, or social outcasts and people with disabilities approaching Jesus.

People of all ages can be involved in these processions, because people of all ages were involved in the original processions.

To prepare, read the words of the song or Scripture to the children. Decide together what items would help people understand the meaning of the song or event. Creative selection of the following elements will make each procession unique and appropriate to the worship theme:

1. costumes: choir robes, cloaks, animal masks, or street clothes.
2. music: anthems, chants, trumpets, silence.
3. props: palms, cloaks, trumpets, suitcases, animals, banners, candles.
4. timing: slow and plodding, quick and shuffling.

Practice the march while the song is sung so the children will understand the route through the sanctuary and the speed at which they will walk.

On one occasion, eight- to ten-year-old children listened to the Christmas carol, "Some Children See Him." They discussed ways they could visualize the song for the congregation. They decided to dress in costumes as they carried flags and international nativity scenes on trays through the sanctuary while a soloist sang the carol.

For another worship service, the pastor preached about the items that were part of the Passover feast. The children marched through the congregation carrying trays of the Passover elements. A small group sang a Hebrew-style worship song.

Variations:
1. For Thanksgiving, children might carry symbols of things for which they are thankful.
2. Children might carry banners which they made in Sunday school.

Sources: Margie Swenson and teaching team, Shalom Christian Community, Medellin, Colombia, South America. Vicky Love and Susan L. Peterson, Cuautitlán Izcalli Covenant Church, Cuautitlán Izcalli, Mexico.

● BIBLE DRAMA

Invite children to dramatize a familiar Bible story that relates to the sermon topic, while an adult or older child reads a modern version.

Prepare by learning about a Bible character or spiritual trait. Tell the children about it through a modern version of the story. With the children, decide how to dramatize the story: Who will play different roles, and how will they use looks and gestures to express actions and attitudes? Working together on costumes will help the children learn about the customs of Bible times. As you construct sets together, the children will learn what the Holy Land is like. Practice the drama several times so that children are comfortable with their roles. Present the drama as part of congregational worship.

Eight- to ten-year-olds might dramatize the Arch book, *Jesus Rides into Jerusalem*, which tells how Jesus entered the city on a donkey. The drama might be presented during worship on Palm Sunday.

Ages: four years and up.

Variations:

1. Older children or youths might memorize their dramatic parts; although the idea is not necessarily to put on a play, memorization may add more drama and realism.
2. For younger children, sets and costumes can be kept simple. For older children, or if your congregation has someone with experience in the theatre, more elaborate or realistic sets and costumes could add to the experience.

Resources:
Petitucci, Karen. *Ministering in Drama for Worship.* San Jose, CA: Resource Publications, 1989.
Smith, Judy Gattis. *Drama Through the Church Year.* Colorado Springs, CO: Meriwether Publishing, Ltd., 1984.
Smith, Judy Gattis. *Twenty-six Ways to Use Drama in Teaching the Bible.* Nashville, TN: Abingdon Press, 1988.
Sources: Margie Swenson and Shalom teaching team, Shalom Christian Community, Medellin, Colombia, South America; Baxter Swenson, First Covenant Church, Denver, Colorado.

● PUPPETS AND MUSIC

Use a Scripture story from one of the Bible readings and music as a basis for creating a puppet presentation. Avoid the use of puppets simply to "preach" at the congregation. Puppets can open a story with drama and lead to new insights.

Look for songs that are related to a specific theme or biblical concept. Practice the song several times with the children. Ask children to draw their ideas about the characters in the song. Provide materials for the children to create puppets (such as stick puppets, hand puppets, or marionettes) for their characters in the song. Practice the song so children are able to sing and move their puppets correctly at the same time.

For example, puppets may be made of foam and painted to represent the different animals in the song, "If I Were a Butterfly." Children sing the song while different puppets move to the music: the bird flies, the elephant lifts its trunk, the worm wiggles, and so forth. The sermon theme might be about the variety in the body of Christ and the value of each member of the church.

Ages: two years and up.

Variations:

1. Older children could make more complex puppets, although the simplicity of the foam hand puppets may be part of the effectiveness of the presentation.
2. Children could teach the song to the entire congregation.
3. Tape record the song and, if you have a sound system, use it to play the song so everyone can hear the music. Children then simply move the puppets at the correct time.
4. Use puppets made of cloth with faces drawn on them; paper sacks; socks; wooden spoons; paper plates; or papier-mache creations.

Source: Margie Swenson and teaching team, Shalom Christian Community, Medellin, Colombia, South America.

SHADOW PLAYS

The story is presented through shadows created by one or more actors who speak and stand behind a sheet or screen in front of the chancel. A bright light *behind* the actors shines toward the sheet, which then creates the shadow seen by the congregation. No costumes are necessary. Props can be created from anything, since the audience sees only their shadows. Here is an example of a brief shadow play.

MIRIAM SPEAKS

Props: flowing fabric to create an image of a costume, large basket, tambourine.

Reader: (Breathlessly) We saved the basket! (A woman or girl in a long, flowing dress holds a basket up so its shadow is cast on the screen.) It was so long ago. When my brother, Moses, was born, the law said we were supposed to throw him into the river to die . . . but my mother couldn't do that. She wanted to obey God. We tried so hard to keep him from crying, but someday, someone was sure to hear him. When my mother knew we could no longer hide him, she put him in a little basket, made of bulrushes. (They are plants that grow along the river.) She put the basket near the river's edge and wedged it into the weeds so it wouldn't drift away. And she put it near the place where the princess came to wash in the water. I remember that the princess said, "Oh, a little baby crying. We must take care of him!" And I was standing nearby, so I could suggest that she ask my mother to be the baby's nurse! It all worked out so well! (The girl steps across the floor and places the basket on the floor.)

So long ago . . . and so much happened. The Lord used Moses to lead us all away from Egypt. The Lord moved the waters back in the Red Sea, so we could travel through safely and escape the Egyptian soldiers. And the King's horses and chariots and horsemen were drowned in the sea. That was a day of music! (Girl picks up the tambourine so its shadow falls on the screen.) I took a tambourine into my hands and all the women followed me with tambourines and singing! (Girl sings, shakes the tambourine, and dances in a small circle so the shadows fall on the screen.)

Sing to the Lord, for he is highly exalted.
The horse and its rider he has hurled into the sea.

Ages: four years and up.

● CLOWNS

Floyd Shaffer notes that occasionally during a worship service in the twelfth century, a door to the chancel area would open and a clown would come in to interrupt the service. This was a "holy interruption" that was used as a consciousness-raising event. The clown arrived, conveyed a message, and left quickly. Worship continued, with a new awareness.

Clowns are filled with Christian symbolism:

1. Paul's letters direct believers to be "fools for Christ's sake."
2. The word *silly* once meant blessed, innocent, holy.
3. The word *simple* once meant uncomplicated and single-minded.
4. Clowns take the values of the world and turn them around to value child-like qualities.
5. The word *clown* comes from the word *clod* . . . and God created human beings from "clods" of earth.
6. Clowns transform the simple into complex meanings and the complex into simple meanings.

Clowns become parables as they share Scripture truth and invite people to respond. Clowns can share a lot in simple ways by sharing the Word in action. Use clowns to illustrate various Scripture stories. Here is an example of a clown skit.

SIMON, SON OF JOHN, FEED MY SHEEP
John 21:15-17

This clown skit follows a sermon that emphasizes serving Jesus through serving others. Two youths or adults are clowns who perform the skit in mime. The first clown, wearing a large nametag that says "Pete," walks into the chancel area with props for doing some kind of work, perhaps carpentry, fishing, or sewing. Pete works for a while. The second clown, wearing a large nametag that says "J. C.," walks into the chancel area. J. C. walks over to Pete and gets acquainted by shaking hands and inviting him to play. Together, they walk with arms around the other's shoulders, play (invisible) frisbee and leapfrog, help each other over rough spots, and point out wonders in the sky.

Then J. C. indicates that he will have to leave. Pete protests. J. C. brings out a balloon—either heart-shaped or with the word "love" written on it in large letters. J. C. points in a questioning manner to Pete, then the balloon, then to himself, as if to say, "Do you love me?" Pete nods enthusiastically. J. C. points to Pete, then the balloon, then to the congregation. Pete looks puzzled. A second time, J. C. points in a questioning manner to Pete, then the balloon, then to himself, as if to say, "Do you love me?" Pete again nods enthusiastically. J. C. points to Pete, then the balloon, then to the congregation. Pete looks puzzled again. A third time, J. C. points in a questioning manner to Pete, then the balloon, then to himself, as if to say, "Do you love me?" Pete looks disappointed that J. C. seems to not believe him and nods gently. And again J. C. points to Pete, then the balloon, then to the congregation. J. C. leaves the balloon in Pete's hand and walks away as he waves to Pete.

Pete stands looking sadly in the direction in which J. C. left. He looks up at the balloon. He looks toward J. C.'s direction. Still sad, he looks up at the balloon. Then he notices the congregation. His face brightens as if he thinks, "Ah-ha!!" and he walks down to someone in the congregation. He hands the balloon to the person in the pew and gives him or her a big hug. Then he indicates that the person should pass the balloon on to the next person, and so on around the congregation, so that everyone gets to hold the balloon as they receive a hug. While the balloon is passing, Pete also leaves.

Ages: three years and up. (Younger children may be hesitant or fearful about clowns in costume.)

Variations:

1. Have a group of helpers available to bring in enough balloons so each person in the congregation can take one home.
2. With another theme, include several clown characters around the congregation. Each one can interpret the sermon images and stories in a different way.

Resources:
Litherland, Janet. *The Clown Ministry Handbook.* Colorado Springs, CO: Meriwether Publishing, Ltd., 1982.
Perrone, Stephen P. and James P. Spata. *Send in His Clowns.* Colorado Springs, CO: Meriwether Publishing, Ltd., 1985.
Shaffer, Floyd. *If I Were a Clown.* Minneapolis, MN: Augsburg Publishing House, 1984.
Toomey, Susan Kelly. *Mime Ministry.* Colorado Springs, CO: Meriwether Publishing, Ltd., 1986.

THE LORD'S SUPPER

Children are too often excluded from the meal that Jesus Christ commanded us to follow in order to celebrate our oneness. This section shows how children can be included in several ways. Children can help bake the bread for communion, or be invited forward to the communion table to receive a blessing from the pastor. Refer to the bread and the cup of the Lord's Supper in simple terms.

● BLESSINGS FOR CHILDREN AT HOLY COMMUNION

Families are encouraged to keep their children with them during the service of Holy Communion. Children can be invited forward with the adults when everyone comes to the altar or chancel area. When the children are included, all ages benefit more from the experience. Church practices vary considerably among the denominations. In many congregations, the worship leader touches children gently on their heads or shoulders and says the words of a blessing. Children may be told ahead of time if they are to receive a blessing or told how to hold out their hands if they are to receive the bread and the cup.

Children in the congregation vary in character. Some are shy. Some are afraid. Some are very outgoing. Leaders can observe the child's body language and keep the child's specific situation in mind to find clues for the blessing to give the child. For example, a child who clings to a parent can receive a blessing which focuses on how good it is to be loved and that points out that Jesus, too, loves the child. Most children will look into the leader's face and listen intently. They may even acknowledge in some way what was said.

Blessings may be based on scripture, such as these adaptions from Numbers 6:24-27:
- The Lord bless you and keep you and give you peace. Amen.
- The Lord make his face shine upon you and be gracious to you. So be it.
- The Lord turn his face toward you and give you peace.
- The Lord make his face shine upon you and put his name on you. Amen.
- The Lord bless you and turn his face toward you.

Variations:
1. Adopt other blessings found in scripture, e.g., 1 John 3:1.
2. Include the child's name in the sentence.
3. Hold the child's hand, rather than touch the head.

Ages: infants and up.

Source: Rev. Duane Cross, Roseville Covenant Church, Roseville, Minnesota.

● LOVE FEAST

The love feast was a family-oriented meal used by the early church and continued by some Christians' traditions, such as the Moravians. The love feast helps Christians remember meals that Jesus shared with the apostles. It can be an expression of Christian fellowship as we meet as the "household of faith."

This practice may be a supplement for the sacrament of Holy Communion that is more inclusive of children and noncommuning members of the Christian community. The love feast, therefore, bridges the walls between rich and poor, divided Christians, social and racial groups. The love of Christ is acted out and celebrated in the feast. Sometimes this is called an agape (Ah-gah´-pay) feast because in Greek *agape* means unconditional love.

The love feast includes an actual meal. Many persons bring food to the table for everyone to share, and people share tasks of serving and leading. There is confession of sin, confession of faith in Jesus Christ, offering, singing, readings, and discussion. There is the breaking together of the bread and the giving of thanks for God's gift, Jesus Christ.

Since the love feast is intended to unite Christians, each person should be personally welcomed by a host.

Ages: infants and up.

Source: *The Worshipbook: Services and Hymns*, Philadelphia, PA: Westminster Press, 1972, pp. 62-64.

Order for an Agape Feast

Let the leader say: Give thanks to the Lord of lords; God's love is everlasting!

A hymn of praise or thanksgiving may be sung, after which the leader may greet the people, welcoming them as friends in Christ.

A reader reads Luke 9:12-17. The leader shall pray:

Let us pray. Great God, whose Son Jesus broke bread to feed a crowd in Galilee: we thank you for the food you give us. May we enjoy your gifts thankfully, and share what we have with people on earth who hunger and thirst, giving praise to Jesus Christ, who has shown your perfect love. Amen.

Have five loaves of bread available. The leader may break one of them, and, after taking a piece of bread, may pass the broken halves, one to the left and the other to the right. The remaining loaves may be distributed to all the people.

Then the people can eat the bread and pass their dishes of food. People may talk together as neighbors in faith, or the leader may direct their conversation by suggesting matters of mutual concern.

When the meal is ended, a reader may read one or more of the following passages, or some other appropriate lesson from Scripture: Matthew 22:34-40; Luke 14:16-24; 1 Corinthians 13; 2 Corinthians 9:6-15.

Then let the leader say:

Let us pray. We praise you, God our creator, for your good gifts to us and all people. We thank you for the friendship we have in Christ; and for the promise of your coming kingdom, where there will be no more hunger and thirst, and where all people will be satisfied by your love. As this bread was once seed scattered on earth to be gathered into one loaf, so may your church be joined together into one holy people, who praise you for your love made known in Jesus Christ, the Lord. Amen.

My dear people, we are all children of God. God's commandments are these: that we believe in his Son, Jesus Christ, and that we love one another. Whoever keeps God's commandments lives in God and God lives in him. We know God lives in us by the Spirit God has given us.

My dear people, since God loved us so much, we too should love one another. No one has ever seen God; but as long as we love one another, God will live in us, and God's love will be complete in us.

The people may sing the doxology.

Then, the leader shall say:

Let us show our love for our neighbors.

The leader may wish to announce a particular need to which the people may give. Offering baskets may be passed around the table so that the people may contribute. A hymn may be sung while the offering is being received or afterwards.

The Lord's Prayer shall be prayed.

The agape feast may conclude with a dismissal:

Go in peace. The grace of the Lord Jesus Christ be with you all. Amen.

SERMONS

Worship leaders need to design sermons to include people of all ages by using simple and direct language. Since one researcher found that the average vocabulary of a congregation is at a seventh grade level, sermons that are clearly worded are more likely to be well received. One example of an inclusive sermon is found in Appendix 2 on page 72. Here are some guidelines for Sunday morning sermons that will appeal to both children and adults.

1. Include illustrations from the lives of children which respond to the needs and questions of children. Mention children in the sermon.

2. Use concrete, specific language. If complex concepts are presented, such as salvation or repentance, use short, concrete definitions and applications.

3. Communicate the way Jesus did: with storytelling, questions, symbols, vivid images, and limited length.

4. Pause before reading Scripture to allow children to find and follow along in their own Bibles.

5. Clearly associate special events (such as communion, baptism, Good Friday) with symbolic objects (such as the communion table or altar, baptismal font, cross).

6. Use stories from children's literature as sermon illustrations. For example, *The Velveteen Rabbit* might be used as an example of new birth and new life.

BIBLICAL NAMES

Scripture and Christian tradition use many names that are chosen for their meaning to that person. For example, Abraham means "father of many nations." John means "God is gracious." Immanuel means "God with us." Persons in some cultures, such as American Indians and Southeast Asians, follow similar customs. Sometimes they might change their name when something significant occurs in their lives.

Choose a biblical name and refer to its meaning and symbolism during the Scripture reading or during the sermon. How would you share the meaning of the name with others? with children? What does it feel like to live with the meaning of a name?

Ages: four years and up.

Variations:

1. Select several names of children in the congregation. Look up the meaning of their names in reference books. Their names might mean something special about them or something their parents hoped for them.

2. Have several people share how they got their names. What did their names mean in their families? Would they choose the same name for themselves? What they would choose instead?

3. Read Isaiah 43:1. What does it mean that God calls us by name? What does it mean that we belong to God? What difference does that make?

4. As part of a service of baptism, share the meaning of the name of the child or person being baptized.

Resource:

Palmquist, Gayle and John Hartzell. *What's in a Name?* Bloomington, MN: Ark Products, 1983.

BIBLICAL SOUNDS

The Bible tells many stories and uses many symbols that might include sounds:

water	wind	storms	horses	lions	roosters
construction	sheep	whales	musical instruments	eagles	fire

Choose a biblical sound and refer to its meaning and symbolism during the Scripture reading or during the sermon.

Ages: two years and up.

Variations:

1. Play a recording or make sounds that are related to the Scripture. For example: water sounds, such as dripping, flowing, raining, storming; or animal sounds, such as mooing, stomping, squeaking.

2. Play the recording without talking for about one minute. Read the Scripture, with the recording as background. Continue the recording for another minute.

Possible themes: baptism, Jesus calming the storm, Noah's ark, animals in the manger, Psalm 23, Psalm 104:19-26.

SCRIPTURE

Introduce the Scripture readings by explaining difficult or significant words or phrases. Pause before reading Scripture to allow children to find the right place and follow along in their own Bibles. Here are several ways to include children and lay people in the reading of Scripture: card choir, choral reading, reading the Scripture in several languages, and scrolls.

● CARD CHOIR

A card choir uses cards of special colors, with words, or with sections of pictures to form special effects to accompany the Bible story. The cards are divided among the card choir members according to the location of their seats. When the cards are held up to face the congregation, the sections of the cards form the larger "picture" that the congregation sees. The card choir will need a director and some rehearsal so that the choir members select and hold up the correct cards smoothly. The card choir should be seated in the chancel area.

Here are cards for the parable of the good Samaritan, or the good neighbor, Sam (Luke 10:25-37). Notice that at times some of the cards will be blank.

Card Series # 1: Location (card choir members hold their cards close together to show the direction the man was traveling).

A man was going down from Jerusalem to Jericho, when he fell into the hands of robbers.

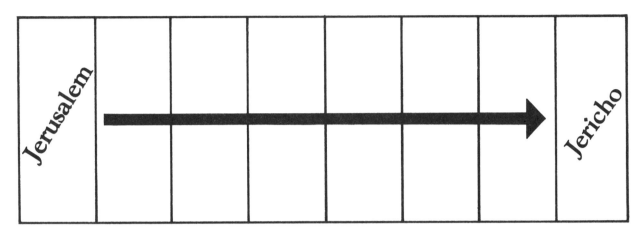

Card Series #2: Words that describe how the man was feeling. After the Scripture is read, each card is turned over as the card choir member shouts out that emotion.

They stripped him of his clothes, beat him and went away, leaving him half dead.

sad	hurt	unhappy	afraid	hopeless	lonely	suffering	anxious

Card Series #3: A priest happened to be going down the same road, and when he saw the man, he passed by on the other side.

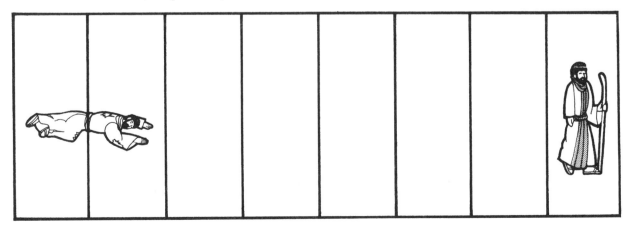

Card Series #4: So, too, a Levite, when he came to the place and saw him, passed by on the other side.

Card Series #5: But a Samaritan, as he traveled, came where the man was; and when he saw him, he took pity on him.

Card Series #6: He went to him and bandaged his wounds, pouring on oil and wine. Then he put the man on his own donkey.

Card Series #7: The Samaritan took him to an inn and took care of him.

Card Series #8: The sixth and seventh cards are covered with silver paper or have silver coins painted on them. All other cards are dark brown.

The next day he took out two silver coins and gave them to the innkeeper. "Look after him," he said, "and when I return, I will repay you for any extra expense you may have."

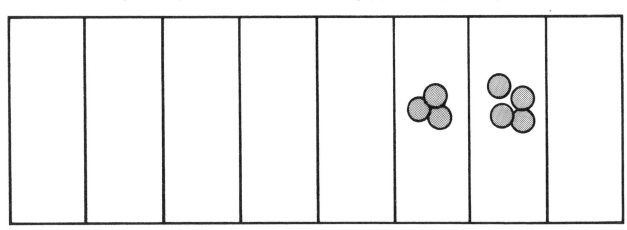

Card Series #9: Cards four, six, and eight show the Samaritan, the Levite, and the priest. All other cards are blank.

Which of these three do you think was a neighbor to the man who fell into the hands of robbers?

Card Series #10: Only the fourth card is shown, that of the Samaritan. All other cards are blank. As the cards are turned over, all the card choir members shout, "Good neighbor, Sam!"

The expert in the law replied (the card choir members join in), "Good neighbor, Sam!"

Ages: two years and up as the congregation; eight years and up as the card choir.

Variations:

1. Any Scripture that could be well illustrated and told as a story.
2. Use contemporary illustrations to personalize the story.

● CHORAL READING

About two weeks ahead of time, line up several people willing to participate in a choral reading. Provide them with the Bible passage for the focus of the choral reading.

Write a choral reading that blends words and sentences for different readers. Create feelings with the words. The participants read or recite the lines assigned to them. There is an emphasis on the group's contributions. Participants' voices are divided into groups: men and women or boys and girls; high and low pitch; solo and group. This might be written as part of a Sunday school lesson and shared with the congregation during worship. Try this with Psalm 136.

All:	Give thanks to the Lord, for God is good.	*Girls:*	Who spread out the earth upon the waters,
Congregation:	God's love endures forever.	*Congregation:*	God's love endures forever.
Adults:	Give thanks to the God of gods.	*Boys:*	Who made the great lights—
Congregation:	God's love endures forever.	*Congregation:*	God's love endures forever.
Children:	Give thanks to the Lord of lords.	*One girl:*	The sun to govern the day,
Congregation:	God's love endures forever.	*Congregation:*	God's love endures forever.
Men:	To God who alone does great wonders,	*One boy:*	The moon and stars to govern the night;
Congregation:	God's love endures forever.	*Congregation:*	God's love endures forever.
Women:	Who by God's understanding made the heavens,	*All:*	Give thanks to the God of heaven.
Congregation:	God's love endures forever.	*Congregation:*	God's love endures forever.

Ages: three years and up.

● SCRIPTURE IN SEVERAL LANGUAGES

The meaning of Scripture is closely connected to language. Originally the Bible was written in Greek, Hebrew, and Aramaic. Now we read it in many different languages. The language that is used can open up the meaning of the Scripture or restrict it if we become boxed into thinking that only our own language gives the right interpretation. Use several other languages as the Bible is read. Perhaps congregational members can read in French, Spanish, Swedish, Chinese, Hmong, or Swahili.

Use Luke 2:1-7, the story of the birth of Jesus, in several languages to emphasize how Jesus came for the whole world.

(*English*) In those days Caesar Augustus issued a decree that a census should be taken of the entire Roman world. (This was the first census that took place while Quirinius was governor of Syria.) And everyone went to his own town to register. So Joseph also went up from the town of Nazareth in Galilee to Judea, to Bethlehem, the town of David, because he belonged to the house and line of David. He went there to register with Mary, who was pledged to be married to him and was expecting a child. While they were there, the time came for the baby to be born, and she gave birth to her firstborn, a son. She wrapped him in cloths and placed him in a manger, because there was no room for them in the inn.

(*French*) En ce temps-là, l'empereur Auguste' donna l'ordre de faire le recensement de tous les habitants de l'empire romain. Ce recensement, le premier, eut lieu alors que Quirinius était gouverneur de la province de Syrie. Tous les gens allaient se faire inscrire, en se rendant chacun dans sa propre ville. Joseph partit de la ville de Nazareth, en Galilee, pour aller en Judée dans la ville appelée Bethléem, où est né le roi David, parce qu'il était lui-même un descendant de David. Il alla s'y faire inscrire avec Marie, sa fiancée. Elle attendait un enfant et, pendant qu'ils etaient à Bethléem, le jour arriva où son bèbè devait naître. Elle mit au monde un fils, son premier-né. Elle l'enveloppa de langes et le coucha dans une crèche, parce qu'il n'y avait pas de place pour eux dans la maison où logeaient les voyageurs.

(*German*) Zu jener Zeit ordnete Kaiser Augustus an, daß alle Bewohner des römischen Reiches in Steuerlisten erfaßt werden sollten. Es war das erste Mal, daß so etwas geschah. Damals war Quirinius Statthalter der Provinz Syrien. So zog jeder in die Heimat seiner Vorfahren, um sich dort eintragen zu lassen. Auch Josef machte sich auf den Weg. Von Nazaret in Galiläa ging er nach Betlehem, das in Judäa liegt. Das ist der Ort, aus dem König David stammte. Er mußte dorthin, weil er ein Nachkomme Davids war. Maria, seine Verlobte, ging mit ihm. Sie erwartete ein Kind. Während des Aufenthalts in Betlehem kam für sie die Zeit der Entbindung. Sie brachte einen Sohn zur Welt, ihren Erstgeborenen, wickelte ihn in Windeln und legte ihn in eine Futterkrippe im Stall. Eine andere Unterkunft hatten sie nicht gefunden.

Ages: eight years and up, depending on language used in the home.

Variations:
1. Have readers whose primary language is different from your congregation's present Bible passages in their own language and then have them present that version translated directly into your congregation's language. During the sermon, focus on differences in the translation.
2. Write to several missionaries in other lands. Ask them about the meaning of biblical terms and stories in the language and cultures of the countries in which they work.
3. Have each reader prepare to read the same Scripture, Acts 2:1-21, but each in a different language. All readers read their Scriptures at the same time. Point out parallels with the scene at Pentecost, when people from all over the world heard the apostles testifying in their own languages.

Possible themes: Pentecost, witnessing
Source: First Covenant Church, St. Paul, Minnesota.

● SCROLLS

Create scrolls from the cardboard rolls from gift wrapping or paper towels. Attach white or brown shelf paper to the rolls. Children can write Bible verses in their own words on the scrolls and read them during the worship service, or a whole story can be put on a scroll. Here is one story that could be used for this purpose. It is adapted fom Exodus 3:1-15.

Exodus 3:1-15

Moses was watching the sheep of Jethro. Moses took the sheep to the other side of the desert, near Horeb, the mountain of the Lord. An angel of God appeared to Moses in flames of fire from a bush. Moses saw that the bush was on fire, but it did not burn up. So Moses thought, "I will go over and see this strange sight—why the bush does not burn up."

When the Lord saw that he had gone over to look, God called to him from within the bush, "Moses! Moses!"

And Moses said, "Here I am."

"Do not come any closer," God said. "Take off your sandals, because this is holy ground. I am the God of your father, the God of Abraham, the God of Isaac, and the God of Jacob."

Moses hid his face because he was afraid to look at God.

The Lord said, "I have seen the sadness of my people in Egypt. I care about them. I will save them from the Egyptians and take them to a safe and good land. I am sending you to the king of Egypt to bring my people out of Egypt."

But Moses said to God, "Who am I, that I should go to the king and bring your people out of Egypt?"

God said, "I will be with you. When you have brought the people out of Egypt, you will worship me on this mountain."

Moses said to God, "What if the Israelites ask me what your name is? What shall I tell them?"

God said to Moses, "I AM WHO I AM. This is what you are to say. 'I AM has sent me to you.' "

God also said to Moses, "Say to the people, 'The Lord, the God of your fathers has sent me to you.' This is my name forever, the name to remember from family to family."

Ages: six years and up.
Variations:
1. Children produce their scrolls as the culmination of a unit of study in Sunday school, or children's choir.
2. Have a group of children read the Scripture. Each one can have a verse or two on a scroll to read.

CREATIVE ARTS

Many people in the congregation can assist in worship by providing creative arts resources. Observe the pageantry of worship when colorful paraments and banners are included. Symbols from the Bible and from the church year will enrich everyone's worship.

● BANNERS

Create banners for the Scripture story and for the understanding of the story's meaning by the group of children.

The banner illustated here was created for the church season of Epiphany. There were five quilted panels with symbols that were to be attached with velcro fastening, one panel added each week during the children's sermon. Week 1: the "Epiphany" panel; Week 2: boxes of gold, incense, and myrrh (Matthew 2:1-12); Week 3: water and a dove (Luke 3:21,22); Week 4: clay jars with wine (John 2:1-11); Week 5: a Scripture scroll (Luke 4:14-21).

The following children's story was presented the first week of Epiphany:

There are many seasons in our Christian calendar. We have just finished the seasons of Advent and Christmas, and now we are in the season called Epiphany. This is the time between Christmas and Lent.

This time is special in our church because we remember that Christ came for the whole world. We remember that Christ was baptized and started his ministry. Epiphany means "to show." That means it is the showing of the glory of God, who sent Christ to the world.

Four things happened to show us that Jesus was Christ, the Savior. The first was the wise men's recognition of Jesus soon after his birth as the king of the Jews. The second was Jesus' baptism by John the Baptist. The third was Jesus' miracle of transforming water to wine at a wedding feast, and the fourth was Jesus' reading from a Scripture scroll about the coming of the Messiah and his comment that now those words had been fulfilled.

These things happened when Christ was sent into the world. So the Epiphany season is a time to emphasize the missionary work of the church. For the next five weeks, we will emphasize Christ's call to us as his people. Each week, a new symbol will be placed on this banner to help us to remember the season of Epiphany . . . the time when Christ showed us too how we can go out into the world to tell people about Christ's love for them.

Ages: four years and up.

Variations:

1. Carry the banner into the sanctuary during the opening hymn.
2. Keep the banner hanging in the sanctuary during the season of Epiphany.
3. When the season is over, give the banner to a nursing home, a shut-in, an elderly friend, or one of the children.
4. Use banner poles to hold up streamers and wind chimes for a Pentecost procession.

Other themes: Easter, Pentecost, Thanksgiving Day, other Bible stories.

Source: Steve and Martha Burger, First Covenant Church, St. Paul, Minnesota.

● BIBLICAL SYMBOLS

Many concrete things mentioned in the Bible take on meaning as signs and symbols: cross, fish, bread, staff in the wilderness, fig, tree, coat of many colors, lamp, harp, animals in the ark, jail cell, gold, Red Sea, crown of thorns, vine, key, crow, burning bush, ship, sun, scroll, candles, light, rooster, dove, rock, rose, water, branch, sheep, lion, lily, cup, coin, eagle, fire, fruit, vine.

Choose a biblical symbol from a Scripture reading to emphasize during the worship service. Whenever possible, bring one or more concrete objects to the service. Refer to the meaning and symbolism during the Scripture reading or during the sermon. Involve the children in carrying the symbols or objects. Think about how to share the meaning of the symbol with others, especially with the children.

Ages: four years and up.

Variations:

1. Wear the biblical symbol. What does it feel like to wear a symbol that others can see? What does it mean to you? What might it mean to others?

2. Include the biblical symbol on a banner to hang near the chancel or at the church entrance. This banner might be prepared by a children's Sunday school class.

3. Draw the symbol and write the Scripture reference with a black marker on a piece of white paper that is about 4″ high by 12″ long. Make copies of this either on plain paper or on adhesive-backed paper to create bumper stickers. Give one copy to each worshiper.

4. Introduce the sermon with a newspaper caption. For example, "Forecast: 40 days and 40 nights of rain."

5. Tell the story from the point of view of the object. What would the burning bush say? What would Paul's jail cell say?

6. Select a symbolic object, such as a branch or a candle. Give each worshiper an object to touch and study. Have each person complete the statement:
   ● "God is like a _____because . . ." or
   ● "The Kingdom of God is like a _____ because . . ." or
   ● "Scripture is like a _____ because . . ."
   Share what you have learned about the topic by exploring the objects.

CHURCH YEAR SYMBOLISM

The worship experience of children and others can be enriched through the symbolism of the church year.

Historically, the Christian church has followed certain practices related to seasons of the church year. For example, expectation was practiced during the season of Advent, penitence during Lent, joy during Easter, and zeal during Pentecost. Observing the church year can nurture the spiritual lives of participants and give variety to tradition and routine. One approach divides the year to focus on events of the life of Jesus Christ: Advent, Christmas, Epiphany, Lent, Holy Week, Easter, Ascension, and Pentecost.

Many denominations have assigned a color and symbols to each season. On page 67 is one church's calendar.

SEASON and COLOR	MEANING	SYMBOL	MEANING
Advent Blue	Hope and faith	Jesse tree	Jesus' descendence from Jesse. Is 11:1
		Rose	The earth will bloom with joy. Is 35:1
Christmas White	Celebration	Manger	The crib for baby Jesus. Lk 2:7
		Angel	Angels sang at Jesus' birth. Lk 2:8-14
		Staff	First visitors at Jesus' birth. Lk 2:8-20
Epiphany White Green	Celebration and joy New life and hope	5-point star 3 boxes candle	The star of Bethlehem. Mt 2:1-10 The gifts from the Magi. Mt 2:1-11 Simeon's song. Lk 2:29-32
Ash Wed. Purple	Penitence	Ashes	Grief and penitence. Lk 10:13
Lent Purple	Penitence	40	Jesus' temptation period. Lk 4:1-2
Palm Sun. Purple	Penitence	Palms	Waved at Jesus' arrival. Jn 12:13
Maundy Thursday Purple	Penitence	Chalice and bread Grapes and wheat	Food at the Last Supper. Mt 26:20-30
Good Fri. Black	Mourning	Crown of thorns Cross	The crown at crucifixion. Mk 15:16-20 Jesus' cross. Mk 15:24.
Easter White	Celebration and joy	Lamb or banner Empty tomb Victory crown Butterfly or lily	John's vision of Jesus. Jn 1:29 Jesus' resurrection. Jn 20:1-16 Given to believers. 2 Tim 4:8 Resurrection of the body. 1 Cor 15:35-56
Pentecost Red	Fire and sacrifice	Dove Flames	The dove at Jesus' Baptism. Mk 1:9-11 Arrival of the Holy Spirit. Acts 2:1-4
Trinity Green	New life and hope	Triangle	God, Jesus Christ, and the Holy Spirit

Ages: infants and up.

Variations:
1. Use the colors and symbols in clergy vestments, chancel decorations, flowers, banners, bulletin boards, worship bulletins.
2. Use concrete objects for the symbols, such as candles during Advent, a crèche scene at Christmas, star mobiles at Epiphany, palm branches on Palm Sunday, a cross of two nails on Good Friday, lilies at Easter.
3. Select hymns that relate to these symbols.
4. Include sermon illustrations that refer to these concrete symbols. Define the words and concepts in the sermon.
5. Use the colors and symbols in the children's activity bulletins.

Source: First Covenant Church, St. Paul, Minnesota.

● TREE OF CROSSES

Select a strong tree branch or save a short Christmas tree (remove the needles). Place the branch in a coffee can filled with plaster of Paris. Allow it to harden. Using a book or brochure about crosses as a reference, have children trace or draw different styles of crosses. Cut the crosses out of contrasting colors of construction paper or out of gold or silver foil paper. Punch a hole at the top of each cross and thread a string or ribbon through the hole. Prepare a bulletin insert that briefly describes each style of cross. Beginning on Ash Wednesday, add several crosses to the tree during each worship service during Lent.

Ages: four years and up.

Variations:
1. Each week, have the children who made the crosses read the description of the style of cross and what it symbolizes.
2. Select a different symbol to repeat on the tree. For example, have children create stars during Epiphany or butterflies at Easter.

● QUIET ACTIVITY BAGS

Parents may offer a variety of quiet activities for children to use during the adult-oriented components of the worship hour. Allow children to select three or four items before leaving home and to pack the materials in their own bag, backpack, or purse. As young children use these quiet toys during worship, they receive positive messages about their presence and are included in ways that are appropiate to their developmental level. Reserve the quiet activity materials for use only during the adult-oriented sermon so children may participate in most of the worship hour. Such materials might include:
1. small pocket-size books (use board books for toddlers)
2. three to six crayons
3. scrap paper
4. simple connect-the-dot Bible story pictures
5. write-on/wipe-off books and markers
6. dry, bite-size cereal
7. book of family snapshots
8. letters and numbers cut out of felt

Ages: toddlers and up.

Variations:
1. If worship themes are available in advance, select Bible story books to relate to the theme.

Resources: Arch Books, Concordia Publishing House, St. Louis, MO.

APPENDIX 1

RESPONSES TO CONCERNS AND QUESTIONS

Although children and adults share in a group worship event, they may not share exactly the same experience. Worship is still an individual act that may happen in a group setting. Adults will naturally have questions and concerns about including children in congregational worship. The worship committee and other church leaders will want to respond tactfully and respectfully to these issues. The following are questions and comments that may come up.

1. **What should we look for in a congregational worship service that includes children?**

a. Greetings, prayers, and sermons acknowledge the presence and welcome children in the congregation.

b. Sermons include illustrations from the lives of children and respond to the needs and questions of children.

c. The language of prayers, responses, sermons, and hymns is understandable (that is, concrete) for children. If complex concepts are presented (such as salvation or repentance), short, concrete definitions and applications are provided.

d. Symbolism is used to enhance worship, such as paraments to correspond to the church year, banners, windows, and objects. Symbolism is explained.

e. Worship experiences are provided that use many senses: sight, sound, touch, taste, smell, kinesthetic sense, visceral sense, balance, spatial sense, sense of time, and spiritual sense.

f. Worship experiences are provided in many settings.

g. Children are given their own Bibles, and time is allowed for them to find the Scripture passage and read along.

h. Children learn prayers and responses in Sunday school classes so that they can join in with the congregation.

2. **What about children who cry and talk so loudly that they disturb the entire congregation?**

Realistically, the congregation should provide for children to participate in church life according to their individual needs and abilities. Some children may not be ready for congregational worship. There is still a place for infant and toddler nurseries. In fact, the existence of nurseries also suggests that children are welcome in the community and that their special needs are considered important.

Children are naturally active, so parents and church leaders will want to provide quiet activities for children to use during the parts of the worship service that are more oriented toward adults.

Infants may be "walked" along the wall with windows. The colors of the glass or the scenery may help them calm down. Young children may need to walk up and down the pew or stand on the pew to see better. Parents might want to remove the child's shoes to soften the noise. Other youngsters may want to sit on the kneeler in churches that have them and use the pew for a desk as they write or color.

Parents may provide quiet toys, such as Bible story books, stuffed animals, photo books, crayons and paper, and purses.

Some children will relax with gentle rubs on the back, shoulders, or arms. A small snack may be acceptable, such as a bottle for infants, dry cereal for toddlers, apple wedges or raisins for older children. A snack would be especially helpful on Sundays when Holy Communion is observed in congregations that do not serve the elements to children.

Other options might be made available for children whose parents are not ready to have them in worship. Children's church, infant and toddler nurseries, or children's choir rehearsal might be considered. These options must be developmentally appropriate.

3. Shouldn't children be included in church events beyond congregational worship?

The church's ministry should include family oriented events where children and their natural activity are welcome. Child care should be provided during special adult programs. Parent education and parent support groups may be developed. Counseling should be offered directly to children who experience grief or stress. Church leaders should know children's names and acknowledge important events in their lives, such as birthdays, illnesses, new siblings, or moving.

4. What about the toddler who walks out of his or her family's pew and up and down the aisles?

The worship committee will want to discuss this situation with parents of young children and with the ministerial staff. Some congregations actually welcome short, quiet movements from toddlers. Children who feel free to move a bit might in fact become ministers to those adults whom they approach.

5. Including children in worship seems like a nice idea, but who will take responsibility to lead and plan?

The pastor must endorse the concept, be open, and facilitate the inclusion of children in worship. Then lay people can plan and lead. Including children should be seen as natural and

expected, rather than as an interruption or intrusion. See the description of a worship committee's tasks earlier in chapter 2.

6. But I object to puzzles and games during worship.

The suggestions in this book have been designed to relate the activities of children to the theme or the sermon. The important distinctions are that the activities should be appropriate to the child's level of development; make children comfortable in worship; pass the time constructively during the parts of the service that are more adult oriented.

7. Some parents sing in the choir or lead the service. What about their children? What about children from the neighborhood who attend without their own parents?

One option is to allow the child to sit with the parents in the choir. For children unaccompanied by parents, you might find an adult friend, a Sunday school teacher, or a relative with whom the child may sit.

8. We don't want to be just "cute."

Adults seem to value order and ritual, the routine of the expected. Leaders who plan worship experiences do need to be theologically responsible. Worship with skits and musical performances that are designed simply to attract an audience may be unable to nourish and inspire the people in their response to God. Therefore everything that is planned needs to be integretated into the themes and purposes of the worship service.

APPENDIX 2

AN EXAMPLE OF AN INCLUSIVE SERMON: OFFER YOURSELF IN LOVE
ROMANS 12:1, 2, 9–21

by Elizabeth J. Sandell

INTRODUCTION

The book of Romans was important to me as a teenager. It includes big concepts such as salvation, justification, and sanctification, but it helped me with questions like: Who is Jesus? How can I find God? Why do I do things I don't want to do? What if we can't be good enough? How can we escape the consequences of our wrongdoings? What about people who haven't had a chance to hear about Christ? The book of Romans helps us develop a clear picture of what we believe, how our beliefs relate to the rest of the world, and how to bring order to the way we live because of our faith.

Last week, we were encouraged to offer our gifts first to God and then to offer ourselves to others. This week, we are continuing our emphasis on God's gifts to the church as we expand on the remaining section of chapter 12, the beginning of five chapters that provide practical advice on specific problems about the proper focus of our relationships with others both inside and outside the church.

LOVE (ROMANS 12:9-21)

First, "Love must be sincere." Agape love is characteristic of Jesus Christ. Agape love is authentic, real, without ulterior motive, with no hypocrisy. Agape love includes all three aspects of the human personality: heart, soul, and mind. Agape love is not an impulse arising out of feelings. It is not directed toward only those we like. It is not always a natural inclination. Agape love is not hypocritical. It is an outward expression of deep inside honesty, humility, grace, and tact. Agape love is not discriminating. It rejects evil at every turn and supports good in every way.

There are many examples of agape love in the Scriptures. Ruth showed agape love when she stayed with Naomi and went to a foreign land. They were unlikely friends because they were of different generations, different ethnic and religious cultures, and they were mother-in-law and daughter-in-law! But the bond of love held them together.

Jonathan showed agape love as David's friend. They also were unlikely friends because they were of different economic and social classes. David was a shepherd; Jonathan was a king's son. Jonathan's father wanted to murder David, but Jonathan saved David's life because of the bond of love.

Romans 12 teaches us that the proper use of our spiritual gifts in the body of Christ requires this genuine, sincere, other-directed love. Look at the verbs in verses 9 through 21. Love means to be, to give, to keep, to seize, to rejoice, to persevere, to share. Love requires action, sacrificial involvement in the lives of others. The bond of love is the intentional act of laying one's life down for the one who is loved. We need to get serious about acting out that love. It cannot be genuine if we don't actually give it away.

A PARABLE

Think about three things that you really value. The kind of things that you would really miss if you lost them. Your house. Your car. Your dog or horse. How about your china cabinet or the photo albums you started when you were nine years old? Or maybe it would be your child, husband, friend, parents?

For me, something I really value is my grandmother's ring. She received it when she graduated from the eighth grade. She gave it to me about 15 years ago as something to remember her by. It was a large size and the band had nearly worn through, so I had it repaired and resized. Once I thought that I had lost it and I was nearly hysterical.

I want to share this ring with you today. Lauren, would you please come up here to look at it and try it on. I hope you enjoy it. Now, would you pass it to the person next to you so he can enjoy it. And please keep passing it all around the congregation so everyone gets to hold it a while. Later at the sanctuary door, I will give you another ring that you can keep to remember this story when you go home.

Now, while my grandmother's ring goes around the congregation, think about your list of valued things. Could you give those things up out of love? Whatever was on your list, how does it compare with the way you value your body? Or the way you value the "inner you" which that body houses? Maybe you could give away everything else but still hang on to that one most valued possession—yourself.

That's what Jesus really required . . . ourselves. Are we willing to give away ourselves? This is very difficult. John Powell, in *Why Am I Afraid to Tell You Who I Am?* wrote: "I am afraid to tell you who I am, because if I tell you who I am, you may not like who I am, and it's all that I have."

It's difficult to expose our real selves, but we look for that kind of agape love from others.

Steve Winwood, a contemporary musician our young people will recognize, wrote a song called "Higher Love" that deals with the subject of searching for a higher love. You might want to obtain a copy and think about what the words mean.

We look for agape love instinctively. Young people get upset when the church doesn't fulfill this need, and sometimes they join cults. Their own religion let them down and didn't give them something to live up to.

A How-to List

Living agape love in action is not necessarily simple. Let's study this passage carefully. Contemporary musicians like Steve Winwood can help us ask the questions. . . . Paul's letter to the Romans will help us get the answers.

Magazine articles have titles like: "How to catch a northern pike" or "How to make a wardrobe from just two pattern pieces" or "How to make a million dollars in real estate." The list of commands found in verses 9 through 21 is a "how-to list" that makes up the most complete set of directives for Christian living found anywhere in one section of the New Testament.

At our staff devotions time last Wednesday morning, we responded with, "Whew! That's a lot to do!" To be serious about being a Christian, you could almost quit. Only those totally committed to Christ and filled with Christ's Spirit can hope to love in this way. It's the life of Christians at their best.

So, what do we do? That's my kind of question. You know how I am . . . my daily calendar organizes and motivates me to do more so I can cross off the next thing on my list. Paul encourages the use of gifts and follows with a list of things to do in order to minister out of love. Paul's list tells us "how to love." It's a practical list, meant for relationships between individuals, and it's an attainable list, because the Holy Spirit will empower us.

In Romans 12, Paul suggests many things organized into four categories:
1. our attitude toward God
2. our attitude toward ourselves
3. our attitude toward other believers
4. our attitude toward our enemies

Our attitude toward God is to be one of service in love: "serve the Lord . . . never flag in zeal, be aglow with the Spirit." We are not to shrink or hesitate in our service to God. We are to be enthusiastic, diligent, and fervent, even to the point of singing in the Spirit. "Rejoice in your hope, be patient in tribulation, be constant in prayer." Our joy is from our hope in Christ. We are to be steadfast, constant, faithful, and have endurance and perseverance in all afflictions, distresses, sufferings, and pressures.

Our attitude toward ourselves is to be one of acceptance and humility:
a. acceptance of who we are as God created us and gifted us
b. humility of spirit—not thinking too highly of ourselves and our own efforts

Our attitude toward other believers is to be one of love with family affection. God's love is supposed to be exercised with believers—devoted, full of tenderness, and with family affection.

"Outdo one another in showing honor." This is how we are supposed to love one another, with unselfishness and preference for the others. The strong and popular are not supposed to control the life of the faith community. Too often, we have hesitated to associate with someone of lower position. They were too young, too old, less talented, less wealthy, less attractive, of another race. Is a doctor more important than a secretary or a mother? Is a professor more important than a student? How would Jesus judge?

"Contribute to the needs of the saints." We are to meet the needs of other believers. We have responsibilities to each other, here and elsewhere.

"Practice hospitality." Hospitality is the love of strangers. We are to pursue friendliness.

Our attitude toward our enemies is also to exemplify agape love.

"Bless those who persecute you; bless and do not curse them." Believers are expected to counteract their natural, human tendencies to lash out, and instead we are to be gracious. "Rejoice with those who rejoice, weep with those who weep." We are to empathize, to put ourselves in the other's place, to see the other's point of view, rather than defending ourselves.

"Live in harmony with one another" may not always be possible, but we are to look for the good and encourage good qualities.

"Repay no one evil for evil . . . take thought for what is noble in the sight of all . . . never avenge yourselves, but leave it to the wrath of God." Let God's timing exonerate us, rather than retaliate. "If your enemy is hungry, feed him; if he is thirsty, give him a drink." Believers should expect to meet the other's needs, even if the other is the enemy. We should respond with love.

There are many things to do! What will happen if we take these actions because of our sincere agape love?

There will be difficulties for those who sacrifice themselves. Chapter 12 of Romans warns us of persecution, sadness, and temptation.

By blessing our enemies, returning evil with good, being helpful, and praying, we will heap burning coals on the enemies' heads. This refers to a mideastern ritual in which a person showed repentence by carrying a pan of burning charcoal on the head. If we return evil with good, we will give our enemy a burning sense of shame.

Love in action changes people . . . those who are giving love as well as those who are receiving love: the community of faith and the world.

RETURNING TO THE PARABLE

Let's think about what happened to us because I shared my grandmother's ring. Would the person who has it please bring it up to me? Thank you.

I was scared and afraid to share. I was afraid that my grandmother's ring would be dropped or stepped on or not returned. I wondered if you would really care and be responsible about examining it. I wondered if you would accept or reject the idea or react with apathy or disdain. I considered replacing the ring with something else or just pretending that we had passed it around. I thought about just passing it around the choir, as if they might be more trustworthy. The change that I experienced was that I took the risk of sharing my grandmother's ring. I made the message more important than the ring, and I entrusted the ring to God. Thank you for being so careful.

Let's draw some parallels.

Do we share ourselves with fear, or with abandonment, trust, and love?

Do we substitute other things, like money and status, for love and giving ourselves?

Is it easier to give or to receive?

Do we trust enemies and strangers with ourselves?

If we only trusted some people, would others feel left out?

When we share, do we expect something in return?

GIVING OURSELVES IN LOVE

What encourages us to give ourselves in love?

1. We can choose to love—to obey Christ's command to show agape love, we choose to be willing to be involved in Christian service. For example, Barb Westerhoff demonstrates this. She is a professional working woman who has consciously chosen to take time each Wednesday to be on the team to prepare the All-Church Night dinners. She pours the coffee (regular and decaffeinated) and milk and juice. She has an

attitude of caring that communicates itself to those who have come for the meal.

2. We can decide to take the risk, in spite of inexperience and fear of making mistakes as a new teacher or helper. Helen Bergfalk took the risk of serving as a deacon and visiting others. She was afraid that they might be too demanding or rejecting or misunderstanding. She found that visitation and caring was an exciting ministry for her gifts.

3. We can serve out of our fullness from salvation in Jesus Christ. We can accept the gifts we have been given and overcome our insecurities. Dick Johnson has come to terms with the gifts of teaching and exhortation that God has given him and he serves in Bible Study Fellowship, our Building Planning Committee, and in teaching an adult Sunday school class.

CONCLUSION

Jesus Christ lived and died for each one of us. Jesus considers each one of us to be of immeasurable worth. We can value ourselves and value others enough to offer ourselves in love. Say "yes" to the gifts which God has given us—accept ourselves as God created us. And then say "yes" to the call God has given us—offer ourselves in love in service to others.

Jesus Christ came to serve, not to be served. Jesus gave his life to save people. And we are to love one another as Jesus loved us. Jesus commanded the disciples to give, to love, to lose themselves. He decreed that the first among the disciples was to be the slave of others. He taught that those who surrender their lives will find them.

Hear the good news from John 15:12-17: "My command is this: Love each other as I have loved you. Greater love has no one than this, that he lay down his life for his friends. You are my friends if you do what I command. I no longer call you servants, because a servant does not know his master's business. Instead, I have called you friends, for everything that I learned from my Father I have made known to you. You did not choose me, but I chose you and appointed you to go and bear fruit—fruit that will last. Then the Father will give you whatever you ask in my name. This is my command: Love each other.

Since it is this ministry of servanthood that Christ continues through the church, every function of the body of Christ should be of service. The important thing is not the attention we get or the level of greatness we reach. The church exists for the sake of others. We are to offer ourselves in love.

BIBLIOGRAPHY

BOOKS AND RESOURCES

CHILDREN IN CONGREGATIONAL WORSHIP

Bailey, Robert W. *New Ways in Christian Worship.* Nashville, TN: Broadman Press, 1981.

Ban, Arline J. *Children's Time in Worship.* Valley Forge, PA: Judson Press, 1981.

Barber, Lucie W. *The Religious Education of Preschool Children.* Birmingham, AL: Religious Education Press, 1981.

Benson, Dennis C. *Creative Worship in Youth Ministry.* Loveland, CO: Group Books, 1985.

Benson, Dennis C., and Stan J. Stewart. *The Ministry of the Child.* Nashville, TN: Abingdon Press, 1978.

Bible in Basic English. London, England: Cambridge University Press, 1965. (A basic vocabulary of 850 English words, plus 150 basic Bible words.)

Bitney, James L., and Suzanne Schaffhausen. *Sunday's Children: Prayers in the Language of Children.* San Jose, CA: Resource Publications, Inc., 1986.

Bradner, John. *Symbols of Church Seasons and Days.* Wilton, CT: Morehouse-Barlow, 1977.

Bruck, Maria (ed). *More Children's Liturgies.* New York, NY: Paulist Press, 1981.

Costello, Elaine. *Religious Signing: The New Comprehensive Guide for All Faiths.* New York, NY: Bantam Press, 1986.

The Covenant Book of Worship. Chicago, IL: Covenant Press, 1981.

Cronin, Gaynell. *Holy Days and Holidays, Vol. 2: Prayer Celebrations with Children.* New York, NY: Harper and Row Publishers, Inc., 1988.

Cully, Iris V. *Christian Worship and Church Education.* Philadelphia, PA: Westminster Press, 1967.

Curly, Ed, and Maureen Curly. *Church Feasts and Seasons.* Dayton, OH: Pflaum Press, 1983.

Daves, Michael. *Young Readers Book of Christian Symbolism.* Nashville, TN: Abingdon Press, 1967.

Fant, Louie J. *Sign Language.* Acton, CA: Joyce Media, Inc., 1977.

Foster, Richard J. *Celebration of Discipline: The Path to Spiritual Growth.* San Francisco, CA: Harper and Row, Publishers, 1978.

Gobbel, A. Roger, and Phillip C. Huber. *Creative Designs with Children at Worship.* Louisville, KY: Westminster/John Knox Press, 1981.

Goldman, Ronald. *Religious Thinking from Childhood to Adolescence.* Boston, MA: Routledge and Kegan Paul, 1968.

Grant, Sandy. *Celebrate the Church.* Elgin, IL: David C. Cook, 1987.

Hanson, Richard Simon. *Worshiping with the Child.* Nashville, TN: Abingdon Press, 1988.

Heller, David. *The Children's God.* Chicago, IL: University of Chicago, 1986.

Huck, Gabe. *A Book of Family Prayer.* San Francisco, CA: Harper and Row, Publishers, 1979.

Huck, Gabe, and Virginia Sloyan. *Children's Liturgies.* Washington, D. C.: Liturgical Conference, 1970.

The Joint Office of Worship for the Presbyterian Church (U.S.A.) and the Cumberland Presbyterian Church. *The Service for the Lord's Day: The Worship of God, Supplemental Liturgical Resource.* Louisville, KY: Westminster/John Knox Press, 1984.

The Joint Office of Worship for the Presbyterian Church (U.S.A.) and the Cumberland Presbyterian Church. *The Worshipbook: Services and Hymns.* Louisville, KY: Westminster/John Knox Press, 1972.

Jones, Stephen D. *Faith Shaping: Nurturing the Faith Journey of Youth.* Valley Forge, PA: Judson Press, 1987.

Lane, Leonard G. *The Gallaudet Survival Guide to Signing*. Washington, D. C.: Gallaudet University Press, 1987.

Lang, J. Stephen. *The Complete Book of Bible Trivia*. Wheaton, IL: Tyndale House Publishers, Inc., 1988.

Larose, Paul F. *Working with Children and the Liturgy*. New York, NY: Alba House, 1981.

LeBar, Mary. *Children Can Worship*. Wheaton, IL: Scripture Press, 1976.

Litherland, Janet. *The Clown Ministry Handbook*. Colorado Springs, CO: Meriwether Publishing, Ltd., 1982.

Litherland, Janet. *The Complete Banner Handbook*. Colorado Springs, CO: Meriwether Publishing, Ltd., 1987.

Lutheran Book of Worship. Minneapolis, MN: Augsburg Publishing House, 1982.

Machado, Mary Kathryn. *How to Plan Children's Liturgies*. San Jose, CA: Resource Publications, Inc., 1985.

Magers, Mary A. *Bible Moments with Motions*. Colorado Springs, CO: Meriwether Publishing, Ltd., Publisher, 1984.

Marshall, Eric, and Stuart Hample. *Children's Letters to God*. New York, NY: Pocket Books, Simon and Schuster, 1966.

McNeil, Jesse Jai. *Minister's Service Book for Pulpit and Parish*. Grand Rapids, MI: Eerdmans Press, 1982.

Miller, Madeleine S., and J. Lane Miller. *Harper's Bible Dictionary*. New York, NY: Harper and Row Publishers, 1961.

Miller, Madeleine S., and J. Lane Miller. *Harper's Dictionary of Bible Life*. New York, NY: Harper and Row Publishers, 1983.

Neufer, Sharon, and Thomas Emswiler. *Wholeness in Worship: Creative Models for Sunday, Family, and Special Services*. San Francisco, CA: Harper and Row, Publishers, 1980.

Ng, David, and Virginia Thomas. *Children in the Worshiping Community*. Louisville, KY: Westminster/John Knox Press, 1981.

O'Rourke, Terrence J. *A Basic Vocabulary: American Sign Language for Parents and Children*. Silver Spring, MD: T. J. Publishers, Inc., 1978.

Palmquist, Gayle, and John Hartzell. *What's in a Name?* Bloomington, MN: Ark Products, 1983.

Pentz, Croft M., and Carter E. Bearden. *Ministry to the Deaf*. New Wilmington, PA: House of Bon Giovanni, 1984.

Perrone, Stephen P., and James P. Spata. *Send in His Clowns*. Colorado Springs, CO: Meriwether Publishing, Ltd., Publisher, 1985.

Petitucci, Karen. *Ministering in Drama for Worship*. San Jose, CA. Resource Publications, 1989.

Pfatteicher, Philip H. *Festivals and Commemorations: Handbook to the Calendar in Lutheran Book of Worship*. Minneapolis, MN: Augsburg Publishing House, 1980.

Post, W. Ellwood. *Saints, Signs and Symbols*. Wilton, CT: Morehouse-Barlow, 1974.

Riekehof, Lottie L. *The Joy of Signing*. Springfield, MO: Gospel Publishing House, 1987.

Riekehof, Lottie L. *Talk to the Deaf*. Springfield, MO: Gospel Publishing House, 1963.

Russell, Joseph. *Sharing Our Biblical Story*. Minneapolis, MN: Winston Press, 1979.

Shaffer, Floyd. *If I Were a Clown*. Minneapolis, MN: Augsburg Publishing House, 1984.

Shiplett, Gary R. *Worship and Hymnody*. Colorado Springs, CO: Meriwether Publishing, Ltd., 1980.

Sloyan, Virginia (ed). *Signs, Songs and Stories*. Washington, D. C.: Liturgical Conference, 1982.

Smith, Judy Gattis. *Drama Through the Church Year*. Colorado Springs, CO: Meriwether Publishing, Ltd., 1984.

Smith, Judy Gattis. *Twenty-six Ways to Use Drama in Teaching the Bible*. Nashville, TN: Abingdon Press, 1988.

Stewart, Sonja M., and Jerome W. Berryman. *Young Children and Worship*. Louisville, KY: Westminster/John Knox Press, 1989.

Taylor, Margaret F. *A Time to Dance: Symbolic Movement in Worship.* Austin, TX: Sharing Co., 1980.

Toomey, Susan Kelly. *Mime Ministry.* Colorado Springs, CO: Meriwether Publishing, Ltd., 1986.

Weems, Ann. *Reaching for Rainbows: Resources for Creative Worship.* Louisville, KY: Westminster/ John Knox Press, 1980.

Westerhoff, John H., III. *Values for Tomorrow's Children: An Alternative Future for Education in the Church.* Philadelphia, PA: Pilgrim Press, 1970.

Westerhoff, John H., III. *Will Our Children Have Faith?* New York, NY: Harper and Row Publishers, 1983.

Westerhoff, John H., III, and William H. Willimon. *Liturgy and Learning through the Life Cycle.* New York, NY: Harper and Row Publishers, 1985.

Winter Festivals. San Jose, CA: Resource Publications, Inc., 1985.

Wolfe, Betty. *The Banner Book.* Colorado Springs, CO: Meriwether Publishing Ltd., 1982.

PERIODICALS

Choristers Guild LETTERS. Choristers Guild, 2834 W. Kingsley Road, Garland, TX 75041, 214/271-1521.

Christian Participation Resources. Contemporary Drama Service, Meriwether Publishing, Ltd., Box 7710 - C8, Colorado Springs, CO 80933.

Family Festivals: Celebrating God's World with Families. Resource Publications, 160 E. Virginia St., #290, San Jose, CA 95112.

Liturgical Arts. Liturgical Arts Society, 521 - 5th Avenue, New York, NY 10017.

Liturgy. Liturgical Conference, 1330 Massachusetts Ave. NW, Washington, D. C. 20005.

Rite Ideas. C. S. S. Publishing Company, 628 S. Main Street, Lima, OH 45804.

Worship. St. John's Abbey, Collegeville, MN 56321.

MEDIA

Christensen, Tom. (Director and Producer). *The Mouths of Babes.* [Film]. Baltimore, MD: Mass Media Ministries, 1984.

Peterson, John. (Director and Producer). *Clowns for Christ: A Demonstration and Discussion of Clown Ministry in the Church.* [Film]. Minneapolis, MN: Augsburg Video Productions, 1984.

Worship and the Arts: Liturgical Dance. A 16mm film that introduces dance and interpretive movement in local church worship. 11 minutes. Available from Augsburg Media Division.

North American Liturgy Resources, 2110 W. Peoria Avenue, Phoenix, AZ 85029.

CHILDREN'S BULLETINS

Abingdon Press, 201–8th Avenue South, Nashville, TN 37202.

Communication Resources, P. O. Box 2625, North Canton, OH 44720.

Shining Star, Good Apple, Inc., Box 299, Carthage, IL 62321-0299.

EDUCATING CHILDREN ABOUT WORSHIP

Avery, Richard, and Donald Marsh. *The Avery and Marsh Songbook.* Port Jarvis, NY: Proclamation Productions, Inc., 1972.

Benson, Peter L., Dorothy L. Williams, and Arthur L. Johnson. *The Quicksilver Years.* San Francisco, CA: Harper and Row, Publishers, 1987.

Cavalletti, Sofia. *The Religious Potential of the Child: The Description of an Experience with Children from Ages Three to Six.* New York, NY: Paulist Press, 1982.

Coe, Joyce. *Jesus Rides into Jerusalem.* St. Louis, MO: Concordia Publishing House, 1987.

Schreivogel, Paul A. *Small Prayers for Small Children about Big and Little Things.* Minneapolis, MN: Augsburg, 1980.

Smith, Judy Gattis. *Celebrating Special Days in the Church School Year: Liturgies and Participation Activities for Church School Children.* Colorado Springs, CO: Meriwether Publishing, Ltd., 1981.

Stewart, Sonja M., and Jerome W. Berryman. *Young Children and Worship.* Louisville, KY: Westminster/John Knox Press, 1989.

Williams, Doris, and Patricia Griggs. *Preparing for the Messiah: Ideas for Teaching/Celebrating Advent.* Nashville, TN: Abingdon Press, 1982.

PERIODICALS

Parish Teacher. Augsburg, 426 S. Fifth Street, Box 1209, Minneapolis, MN 55440.

CURRICULUM

Alleluia Series, Augsburg, 426 S. Fifth Street, Box 1209, Minneapolis, MN 55440, 1981. Sets of resources for children ages three years through senior high school provide opportunities for creative growth and a deeper understanding of traditional worship practices. Each year is coordinated with the three-year lectionary and includes 30 lessons.

Arch Books, Concordia Publishing House, St. Louis, MO. Dozens of Bible story books that present theology in clear and simple ways.

Introduction to Worship, 1986, Little Chapel on the Boardwalk, Presbyterian Church in the U.S.A., Cluster Box 4906, Wrightsville Beach, NC 28480, 919/256-2819. Rachel and Huw Christopher, 919/256-2563. Curriculum to introduce young elementary-age children and their parents to the elements of worship. Includes material about the church seasons, prayer, communion, and baptism.

Room to Grow, Augsburg, 426 S. Fifth Street, Box 1209, Minneapolis, MN 55440, 1988. Resources for children ages three through seven years that help young children learn about their world and their relationship with God and with other people. Over 225 teaching experiences, including worship.

TEACHING ADULTS ABOUT CHILDREN IN WORSHIP

Cavalletti, Sofia. *The Religious Potential of the Child: The Description of an Experience with Children from Ages Three to Six.* New York, NY: Paulist Press, 1982.

Christensen, Tom. (Director and Producer). *The Mouths of Babes.* [Film]. Baltimore, MD: Mass Media Ministries, 1984.

Fowler, James W. *Stages of Faith: The Psychology of Human Development and the Quest for Meaning.* San Francisco, CA: Harper and Row, Publishers, 1981.

Jones, Stephen D. *Faith Shaping: Nurturing the Faith Journey of Youth.* Valley Forge, PA: Judson Press, 1987.

Ortlund, Anne. *Up with Worship.* Ventura, CA: Regal Books, 1982.

Webber, Robert E. *Worship Is a Verb.* Dallas, TX: Word Books, Inc., 1985.

FAMILY WORSHIP

Ehlen-Miller, Margaret and others. *The Gift of Time: Family Celebrations and Activities for Advent, Christmas, and Epiphany.* Wilton, CT: Morehouse-Barlow Company, Inc., 1977.

Ehlen-Miller, Margaret and others. *A Time of Hope: Family Celebrations and Activities for Lent and Easter.* Wilton, CT: Morehouse-Barlow Company, Inc., 1979.

Family Festivals: Celebrating God's World with Families. Resource Publications, Inc., 160 E. Virginia Street, #290, San Jose, CA 95112.

Nilsen, Mary Ylvisaker. *Our Family Shares Advent: Scripture, Prayers, and Activities for Families and Other Communities.* San Francisco, CA: Harper and Row, Publishers, 1980. An Advent calendar.

OTHER REFERENCES

Erickson, Erik. *Childhood and Society.* New York, NY: Norton, 1963.

Kohlberg, Lawrence. *The Psychology of Moral Development.* New York, NY: Harper and Row Publishers, 1984.

Piaget, Jean, and Inhelder, B. *The Psychology of the Child.* New York, NY: Basic Books, 1969.